I cannot recall in recent memory a more hard-hi... struggled to overcome such adversity in her life and emerged as an author to ... could not put **BREAKAWAY** down once I started to read.

Jack Roberts, Cable Radio Network
******

Nadia's story of perseverance, hope, and faith can serve as an inspiration to anyone. Nadia's book takes us on a journey through culture, religion, and gender and shows us first hand the hush-hush treatment of girls in various societies. Perhaps more than anything, Nadia provides hope to victims of domestic violence who are still on the inside, looking out. Nadia's story shows us all that there is a place of hope and love beyond those walls.

Sifu Jeff Larson, founder of Chi for Health
******

Child abuse is a huge problem in the world, stretching from the USA to India to the Middle East. Nadia Sahari's book shows one woman's journey out of torment and torture to a new life as an author and actress. She pursued her dreams and they came true for her.

Rick Anthony, *Hollywood Film Flash*
******

BREAKAWAY opened my eyes to the many obstacles one has to face in an abusive relationship. It has been an honor to have Nadia work on our V-day event knowing all that she has overcome. It is important that men and women educate themselves and take responsibility for bringing awareness to abusive situations. This book is a must read for bringing that awareness.

Emiliano Styles, co-founder of Soulploitation/Acting Up!
******

I have not read a book like **BREAKAWAY** in a very long time. From the smell of cigar smoke that symbolizes how her abuse began to repeated abuse for many years, it takes readers through her nightmare. This book is for anyone who has been abused, but it is also for any human being that wants to feel inspired. If you like to read, get this book. If you don't read, you'll be grabbed if you pick this one up.

Connie E. Curry, author of *Give Me Back My Glory*
******

This story is an incredible true account of the human being's incredible ability to continue and flourish in the face of hopelessness and despair. This book is beautifully written and is impossible to put down. Sahari's story is not an easy one to tell, but she does it with grace and an undying hopefulness that has been such an inspiration to me in my life since finishing this book. The message that this book puts across is an important one! It is a must-read!

Autumn J. Clark, NYC
******

I agree with everybody who says that you cannot put this book down until you finish it. I love this story and the hope it gives to all of us.

Valentina Graham, talent agent, Hollywood, CA
******

BREAKAWAY by Nadia Sahari is a memoir that delivers for those who love real life stories. Nadia means "Hope," and **BREAKAWAY** is about how Nadia survived a lifetime of multiple abuses and abusers. Nadia said, "No more abuse" and meant it. Nadia is an engaging writer. At the end of the book is a list of resources.

As a former child abuse investigator, what I know for certain is that everyone needs awareness of the reality of child abuse or we will never stop it. This is a book worth reading. Thank you, Nadia, for sharing your life and hope in **BREAKAWAY**.

Nadine Laman, author of *High Tide*

This is a truly amazing memoir of a wonderful woman. To know that any one human being could withstand so many dramatic and terrifying situations, tragedies that no one human being can possibly fathom, made my heart go out to her. Her deep connection to her faith pulled her through the darkest of times. I recommend this book to anyone who's ever been through any kind of abuse. It will change your outlook on life!

Allison Elizabeth, Austin, TX
******

Nadia shares her life story with us not only as a personal catharsis, but also as a beacon of hope for abused peoples everywhere. Nadia demonstrates the power we all have to redefine our lives and ourselves. Reading **BREAKAWAY**, I am once again encouraged to dare to dream and forgive.

Lara Nixon, Austin, TX
******

I loved reading **BREAKAWAY** because it taught me how strong someone can be, and also to never give up hope. By sharing her story with the world, Nadia Sahari has made her life story one that will inspire others. I admire her for being willing to do this. I think that everyone should read this book.

Paige Lovitt for *Reader Views*
******

Great book! The fact that Nadia has overcome everything she went through is an inspiration for all. Some people would have given up on life, but Nadia just keeps moving forward with hers. Her positive attitude should be a lesson for all women that have gone through abusive relationships. You CAN break away and begin again. Thank you for this truly beautiful book!

Alicia Schowe, San Antonio, TX
******

I read this book in one night, it is well written but also gives those experiencing abuse hope and a pathway to escape their current situation. Nadia teaches how to forgive and move forward with your life. This is a must read!

Ebony Black, Houston, TX
******

Few people have gone through all the trials and tribulations that Ms. Sahari did and come out on the other side to tell their story. The author is thankfully writing from a place of great healing, having managed to change her life completely despite these hardships. I look forward to seeing Ms. Sahari's indomitable spirit portrayed in a movie version of this book some day, as well as more writing from this author.

Agnes Eva, Austin, TX
******

This is an extremely poignant book dealing with issues many women must overcome. I commend Nadia for coming out with her story so that other women can find hope and encouragement, and that they too, can survive abuse.

Irene Watson, Author of *The Sitting Swing*
******

Every once in a while comes a story that I believe has the power to change history. My prayer for this book is that it may bring the change that is necessary in the world to stop abuse and domestic violence. Bravo, Nadia!!!!!!

Christa Jan Ryan, author of *Silent Screams from the Hamptons*
******

Breakaway

The Road to Freedom

Nadia Sahari

Cedar Leaf Press   San Antonio, Texas

Inquiries should be addressed to

Cedar Leaf Press
17503 La Cantera Parkway
Suite 104-240
San Antonio, TX 78257
www.cedarleafpress.com

Library of Congress Cataloging-in-Publication Data

Sahari, Nadia, [date]

Breakaway: The Road to Freedom / Nadia Sahari

p.   cm.

ISBN 978-0-9820413-0-7 (paper)

Library of Congress Control Number: 2008908232

1. Sahari, Nadia, [date] 2. Memoir—Lebanese—Middle East
3. Women—Rape—Sexual Abuse—Domestic Violence

Revised Edition

Printed in the United States of America
Printed on acid free paper

To all the innocent victims of domestic violence and sexual abuse everywhere

Contents

Part Three: Marital Wars

Prologue

*I*T IS IMPOSSIBLE TO SPEAK OR WRITE OPENLY about abuse without offending someone, especially when the abuser is a member of one's own family. This is particularly true in my culture where family honor is so highly regarded, and it is true whether the abuser is dead or alive. No one wants it to be known that a father or grandfather was anything but a good person.

I respect these feelings. I have had them myself. It is inevitable. At the same time, because abuse is so rampant in our world, I have decided to speak out, hoping that my family, all of whom I dearly love, will understand why I write. I truly believe that my story will inspire many victims of abuse to take heart and take control of their lives, to make whatever move they deem necessary for their own well-being.

I have done the best I can to avoid causing offense by changing the names of all the characters in this book. Only my immediate family will recognize the individuals I am writing about in most cases. Others who find themselves in these pages can hide behind their fictitious names if they are so inclined.

I have had wonderful support from many people during the writing of this book. They applaud my success. They commend me for making choices that changed my circumstances. They are happy to see that I am eager to help others who are in abusive relationships. What wonderful, positive people they are! I sincerely thank them all for their encouragement. There are too many to mention by name. They know who they are.

The experiences I share in this book are all true. For many years, I felt alone with my history of abuse and held my silence. I thought I was the only one who had experienced the traumatic abuses I describe here. Gradually and cautiously, in small groups and in speaking engagements, I began to share some of my experiences with other women. To my surprise, I found that many of them had been victims of sexual or physical assault as well. They often said, "Nadia, you went through so much. My life hasn't been anything like yours, and yet I've struggled to cope. You're such an inspiration to me! You should write a book. I'll bet they make it into a movie."

It has not been easy to take their advice. It has been challenging and sometimes devastating to revisit and relive the pain and suffering of my past, to resurrect scenes of violence, to recapture deeply hidden emotions and to put them into words. The journey took me through many dark valleys of depression during which I could not be productive. That is why it has taken almost twenty-five years to produce this book.

Now is the right time. It is right because more attention must be paid to domestic violence and sexual abuse in America. We can no longer be silent witnesses to the daily oppression of innocent victims whose lives are devastated by abuse. We have just elected a new president, but neither major party made domestic violence or sexual abuse a theme of their campaigns. The media are virtually silent on this important issue as well. Therefore, I appeal to America in general to wake up, stand up, and speak up against abuse.

On the other hand, abuse happens to individuals regardless of gender, typically in private settings and without witnesses. The perpetrator may be male or female. It is so personal that it often does not have a voice. Victims of abuse frequently are too ashamed or too fearful to seek help. I write on behalf of all victims of abuse who need encouragement to seek protection and support. It is my sincere desire that my life story will bring you hope and courage to overcome your fears and find freedom from abuse. You can and you must before it is too late. Be strong, be right, dream big, and be free. Live the life you have imagined!

Acknowledgments

*A*S AN ACTRESS, I FULLY UNDERSTAND THE significance of credits, so it is a pleasure for me to express my gratitude to those who have helped me with this book. All my life I have loved reading, writing, and especially spelling. I gratefully acknowledge all the teachers who encouraged me in school. I loved school, not just because I was free from abuse there, but also for the sheer privilege of learning.

My children know that I have also enjoyed taking pictures, just as I enjoy being in front of the camera. They have endured my obsession at family gatherings for years. I promised them that I would not put their pictures in this book, but it has been a hard promise to keep. They are so handsome, and I appreciate them so much that I always want to show them off. Thanks to them for listening to me talk about my life throughout the years and sharing those years with me. I love them with all my heart.

Finally, I thank my husband for his love and support. He wrote the poems *Horizons* and *A Worm and Her Majesty* as well as selected verses from another poem entitled *Trees* that tie the chapters of the book together. He also helped me proofread the manuscript.

Horizons

There is a land where dreams come true,
Where aspirations old and new
Are realized by but a few
Who dare to make the move.

Like Israel on the Moab plains,
This move is not without its pains,
But the land of promise still remains
To those who make the move.

The obstacles are great and tall
Like giants standing one and all,
But no ill fate will e'er befall
The one who makes the move.

The voices from the other side,
Where souls victorious now abide,
Cry "Blessings great and multiplied
For those who make the move."

Breakaway

It is an act of solemn will
That drives the weary pilgrim till
She sees the hope beyond the hill
For those who make the move.

A pioneer in faith, she makes
One step and then another takes
And soon behind her all forsakes
And dares to make the move.

The land before her now is flung.
Its milk and honey song is sung.
A life anew is now begun
For one who made the move.

Part One

Stolen
Childhood

We are as trees, the sky apart,
From tender roots we take our start
And struggle through uncultured soil
Toward unknown destination.

Grandfather's Room

I WAS A GREGARIOUS FIVE-YEAR-OLD. AT SCHOOL I was a real challenge to my teachers. I just could not stay in my seat. I liked to visit all the other children, one by one, like a politician. I am still like that. I love people and enjoy making new friends. My mother is like that, too. As the saying goes, "The apple does not fall far from the tree."

My socializing eventually forced the hand of my kindergarten teacher. She had no choice. She taped me to my seat! That stopped my travels, but I was still able to talk, so she taped my mouth shut! But it was all for nothing. As soon as she cut me loose, I went right back to having fun with my classmates. I did not have a care in the world at school. How I loved the classroom!

Grandfather's room was a whole different thing. For a long time, what happened in that room kept me from living the life I had imagined.

I can still smell the stench of his cigar. It was on his breath and his clothes when I went to his room at the Dix Hotel. I was sent there at least once a week, starting at the age of five.

I had to take dinner to him. It was customary to do that in our Lebanese culture. If he did not come over for dinner, then it was my parents' responsibility to take it to him. Grandfather had lots of money. He carried a roll of one-hundred-dollar bills about three inches thick in his hip pocket. He did not need our food. He was retired from the Ford Motor Company, and his pension was more than what he needed to live on. Taking food to him once a week was a way for my parents to avoid feeling shame and guilt. It also meant they would avoid a harsh lecture from my grandfather about honoring parents. Catering to him was done for a lot of reasons, including, I am sure, to make him feel cared for.

Dearborn, Michigan, had a small Lebanese community when I was a child. It is much larger now, but, no matter how large the community, the family unit is most important in the Lebanese culture. Like all Arabs, regardless of their nationality, Lebanese Arabs are proud and always concerned about what people say or think about them. They are a very generous and hospitable people. However, they will not be shamed or dishonored by anyone, especially a son or a daughter. Grandfather knew this tradition well. If my parents neglected to send him dinner, he did not hesitate to chastise them for it.

Grandfather lived at the Dix Hotel in one room with just a bed, a dresser, an armoire, and a sink. To get to his room, I had to walk from our house on Ferney Street in Dearborn. The Tuxedo Hotel was at the corner of Tuxedo Street and Ferney, three lots from my house. I would turn right there, walk a block to Wyoming, a very busy street, cross it, turn left, and go one block to Dix Avenue.

The Cunningham Drug Store was at the corner of Dix Avenue and Wyoming Street. A Lebanese restaurant where my grandfather had most of his meals stood next to it on Dix. The dime store was beyond that. There was an entrance to the hotel between the restaurant and the dime store. Past the dime store and a cleaners was a coffee house where men gathered to play backgammon and Basra (a favorite card game among Lebanese) while smoking cigars and the traditional hookah or water pipe. Women were never seen there. Grandfather went there often.

The Dix Hotel was above these establishments. The hotel was a brown brick structure—a tired, old, and dingy building. In addition to daily rentals, the management offered apartments as well as studios like my grandfather's. However, unlike studios today, there was no kitchen. Grandfather used a hotplate to make coffee when he did not feel like going to the coffee house.

The main entrance to the Dix Hotel was on Wyoming Street. Double doors opened to the lobby. From the lobby, I had to climb one flight of stairs to a landing, make the turn to climb another flight to a narrow hallway, turn left, and walk almost to the end of the building before coming to Grandfather's room. It was a long way.

There was a back alley entrance, too, and sometimes Grandfather asked me to take that. I did not understand why. The alley entrance scared me to death. Years later, I learned that it was mostly used as a private entryway for hookers and others who did not want to be seen entering the hotel. I never liked to go there.

I usually went to the Dix Avenue entrance, so I could be outside as long as possible. I did not like being inside the hotel. The door at the Dix Avenue entrance was big and heavy. The top half was glass. I had to set Grandfather's plate on the sidewalk in order to open the door with both hands. I would hold it open with my back to the door, bending down to pick up the plate of food before going in. Sometimes, before I could get in all the way, the door would close quickly and push me in.

Once inside, I faced a steep, concrete staircase. There were at least twenty steps to the second floor, maybe more. I never counted. I was always afraid of climbing those stairs. I would hold on to the handrail as tightly as I could. It seemed I had my life in one hand and my grandfather's dinner in the other. At the top of the stairs was a door to enter the hallway. Through the doorway and to the left, it was a fairly short walk to my grandfather's door.

Breakaway

Grandfather's room was small, dusty, and colorless. His bed was right in front of the door. It was a double bed with a metal headboard and footboard. He glued pennies on both the headboard and footboard with chewing gum. The bed was covered with a faded, worn blanket and two feather pillows. One of the pillows had a big depression in it about the size of his head. The mattress sagged in the middle from too many years of use. A large photograph of President Franklin D. Roosevelt hung above the headboard. Grandfather was a devoted democrat. He was a big fan of FDR.

To the left, pushed into the corner of the far wall, was a large, walnut-stained, wood dresser with porcelain knobs. A square mirror framed in wood sat on the dresser, its top leaning against the wall. A row of pennies affixed with more gum decorated the entire frame. My grandmother's picture was on the dresser. There were other pictures, too—snapshots of Grandfather's lady friends as well as my uncles, cousins, and other family members. Each picture frame had its share of pennies.

Beside the dresser, situated at the foot of the bed just a step away, was an armoire that served as a closet. Grandfather loved clothes. He was a meticulous dresser. His public image was very important to him. He liked to socialize and was well known in the community. He wore suits every day with coordinating hats and shoes. If he chose a black pinstripe suit, he wore black shoes and a light gray hat with a black band to match the pinstripes.

Grandfather kept an old, worn suitcase in the armoire. The suitcase was beige with a black strap in the middle. It was the size of a trumpet case. It held a deep secret in the form of a machete. Grandfather kept the machete, because the blood of someone he dearly loved was still on it.

A small, round, pedestal sink was posted in the corner beside the armoire. Grandfather's shaving mug and brush sat on the sink and next to them a straight razor. A white medicine cabinet with a mirror hung on the wall above the sink. The bathroom was outside in the hallway. All the tenants on the second floor shared the toilet and bath. I never saw that room.

Breakaway

Opposite the door to Grandfather's room, beyond the bed, were three large windows. There were no curtains on the windows and no blinds. Grandfather had privacy because he was on the second floor. There were no other buildings across the alley, no people, and no traffic of any kind. No one could see what was going on inside the room. Besides, the windows were dirty and the sills were high, higher than my head. The radiator was under the windows. In the winter, I could hear it hissing and feel the hot, heavy air in the room. It was so hot I could barely breathe. Grandfather's room had no air conditioning.

Grandfather lived there alone. Despite being sociable, he did not have much company, except for the prostitutes that came to his room. He paid them five dollars for services rendered. Everyone in the Lebanese community knew about his business with the prostitutes. Not that Grandfather tried to hide his conduct. Nor was he criticized for it; people thought that a man of his age who was still having sex was a stud. He was respected by everyone, especially men.

Grandfather was not a big man. He was about five feet ten and very slender. His hair was salt and pepper, mostly pepper, and his eyes were dark brown, small, and squinty. His brows were black and bushy and shaped like a bird in flight.

Grandfather was a Shia Muslim, but he did not practice his religion. He would pray once in a while but he never changed the lifestyle that he loved. He was devoted to gambling and sex.

Whenever I took a meal to him, the routine was the same. I tapped lightly on his door. Grandfather was waiting for me. My mother always called him to tell him that I was on my way with his dinner and to watch for me. When he opened the door, I handed him the plate wrapped in aluminum foil, and before I could turn around to go, he would take my hand, pull me into the room, and lock the door. He always said, "Don't you want to spend a little time with your Jiddo?"

Then he picked me up and placed me on his bed. I clenched my fists. My body became rigid. My mind went numb. I closed my eyes and held my breath. Grandfather raised my dress up to my neck. He pulled off my panties, all the while kissing my neck and blowing hot, stinking air into my ears. He continued kissing me all over, placing his disgusting, cigar-tasting tongue in my mouth and ears. I hated him. I was terrified of him. I hated what he was doing to me. I wanted to run away and never come back, but there was no escape. I wanted to scream but could not. I had no voice. I wished I could fly away, far, far away, even beyond the sky. But I had no wings. I cried and screamed inside, but only inside. There was no outside anymore: "Let me go! Let me go! Please, Jiddo. Please, let me go. Don't hurt me. I want to go home. Please stop, Jiddo." Nobody heard me. There was no one to hear. My voice was silent as it would be for many, many years to come, silent but for the echo in my mind.

I lost all sense of feeling as Grandfather was having his way; there was nothing I could do. First, he rubbed his penis on my private parts. Then he rubbed it on my feet and legs and all over my body. Then back to my privates. Then, just before he ejaculated, he would run to the little porcelain sink and let all the sperm go right there so as not to get any on me or my dress. He always made sure that there were no signs of what he had done.

Before he let me go home, he would take the suitcase from the top shelf of the armoire and remove the machete.

"Do you see these blood stains?" He waved the blade in my face. "If you ever tell anyone about what Jiddo does, your blood will be on this, too. I'll chop you up and put you in this suitcase. No one will ever find you. Do you understand?"

"Yes, Jiddo, please let me go," I sobbed, trembling all over.

Then Jiddo put the machete back into the suitcase. He would show it to me again from time to time. I can still see the blood stains.

After it was all over, Grandfather would give me some small coins or a fifty-cent piece. I was nothing to him, just an object for his perverted desires.

I was absolutely afraid of the machete. It was enough to silence me. I fully believed Grandfather would kill me. I feared that I would never see my family again. I had good reason. As an adult, I heard stories that my grandfather had killed his wife with that same machete. He was insanely jealous over her. My grandparents rented a room to a gentleman. Grandmother was never unfaithful, but when Grandfather discovered that she innocently had gone to a movie with the boarder, he reportedly spied on them at the theatre, followed them home, killed and dismembered both of them with the machete, and burned their parts in the basement furnace. Whether the story is true or not, I do not know. I was told that my grandmother and her friend disappeared, never to be seen again.

I was made to go to Grandfather's room until the age of seven. After that, one of my siblings or one of my cousins was sent, and I was kept busy with other chores around the house. I am not aware that my grandfather molested my sisters. If he did, they have kept their silence. Perhaps they repressed their experiences as I did mine. After many years, I learned that Grandfather did to one of my cousins exactly what he did to me. Molesters will always find a victim.

I eventually left my grandfather's room, but it never left me. I carried it with me in silence most of my life. I still carry it, but not in silence now. In some ways, talking about it has set me free, but it always hurts to know that someone you trusted was the cause of your pain. It is especially true when you are an innocent child and the offender is an adult, worse still a member of your own family. Trust lost in childhood is difficult to regain. My grandfather has been dead for a long time, but the scars he left remain with me. I say scars because in many ways I am healed. The abuse I suffered is no longer an open wound. Exposing Jiddo's deeds now is not easy for me, but I find some strength and freedom in the telling.

Even now, in writing this chapter, my whole body aches, and I feel like I am chained to Grandfather's bed. I have a shooting pain going down my arms and legs. I am gripped again by the need to fly away. I am short of breath. I feel like I am suffocating. I am drained. Exhausted. I smell the cigar once more. The memories are hard to face, but I must move on.

How does one heal from sexual molestation? Healing begins with forgiveness and ends with reconciliation. In order to give myself the freedom to heal and to go forward in my life, I have had to forgive my grandfather for what he did to me. Unfortunately, I never had the opportunity to confront him; he died before I became aware of his acts. My grandfather never acknowledged his evil deeds to anyone, and he never confessed to me or asked for forgiveness. I wish he had. I might have been able to reach the reconciliation stage of healing, and my later years might have been less traumatic.

I have found that healing from sexual molestation is like peeling an onion. The pain is removed layer by layer it seems, and when you think you have removed the last layer, another appears. The layers seem to emerge from deep within the subconscious mind. I just deal with them as they surface. I do not know if the pain ever goes away never to return again.

The inner child of the past lives on. She still needs a lot of nurturing. I embrace her. I talk sweetly to her. I take her by the hand, and we go on together. I have no doubt that the molested little girl within me will well up with emotion again one day when I remember Grandfather's room, but I also know that we will rise above those feelings. We have done it many times before. We will fulfill our dreams.

I find that healing takes place when I turn my eyes away from my grandfather, away from being a victim, away from what he did to me, to what I want to be. As long as I allow my mind to dwell on his room, I still live in bondage to my thoughts. When I break away, I find that I am able to take risks. I am able to make changes. I can move on. Only then can I fly toward my dreams.

Having experienced flying, I know that I can never be ruled by Grandfather's room again. I know that healing, like flying, is a process rather than a single event. It is in fact a metamorphosis. It is like being transformed from a caterpillar in a cocoon to a butterfly. It is easy to step on a worm. It is difficult to catch a butterfly.

Breakaway

Finally, I realize that not all flights are smooth. Turbulence and clouds will come. If you cannot see where you are going, you must rise above the clouds. I know this for certain: when you are flying, it does not matter where you have been. It only matters where you are going. Your dreams are your destination. There is freedom in flying toward your dreams.

'Tis not for us to live as moles,
Confined to subterranean holes.
Roots do not define us all.
There is a higher station.

Kaleidoscope

C HOICE IS MORE IMPORTANT THAN CULTURE. Roots alone do not define the tree nor do they define people entirely. You may be planted in a particular culture, but choices are what make you grow. My roots are Middle Eastern. I have often looked at my life, especially during the years of abuse, and asked: "What if I had been born somewhere else or to someone else? How would my life have been different?" In the end, these questions do not lead to freedom; they reflect the kind of thinking that keeps you in bondage. They show that you are a victim rather than a victor. They look backward instead of forward. They do not help you to realize your dreams.

Roots are what you are given at the start of your life. They are what you cannot change: your DNA, your birthplace, when you were born, who your parents are, etc. All these things are beyond your control. You can never separate yourself from your roots, but in the end they prove to be merely circumstantial. It is what you do with your own life that counts. That is a choice you make.

Breakaway

I was born in a suburb of Beirut, Lebanon. Beirut, a city five thousand years old, is situated on the eastern end of the beautiful Mediterranean Sea. The Beirut I was born into was different than what it is today. It was beautiful then. Beirut was called the Paris of the Middle East and Lebanon the Switzerland of the Middle East. Tourists came from all over the world to vacation there. It was the financial and cultural center of the Arab world. Much of that Lebanon was destroyed in the civil war of 1975-1990. Now Lebanon continues to rebuild, but it is difficult largely because of outside political influences whose intention it is to control the country.

Lebanon is really a melting pot where melting has not occurred. It is a mountainous country with diverse ethnic populations and sectarian religious groups. Arabic is the official language, but French is widely spoken because France governed the country after World War I until its troops finally left in 1946. English is used as well, especially in doing business. My native language is Arabic.

Unlike most Arab countries, Lebanon has a wide variety of religious groups. Approximately half the population claim Christianity as their faith: Maronites (Eastern Catholics), Greek Orthodox, Greek Catholics, Armenian Orthodox, Protestants, and Roman Catholics. As for Muslims, Sunnis and Shia are about equally divided today. Sunnis live mainly along the coast while Shia dwell mainly in the mountains and the northern Bekaa Valley. Among the other religious groups are Copts, Druze, and Jews.

Being at the crossroads of the Middle East, Lebanon has been dominated by various peoples. As far as I know, it has never had an indigenous population. In the third millennium BC, the seafaring Phoenicians made it their home. Then the Babylonians, Egyptians, Hittites, Assyrians, Persians, Greeks, Romans, Arabs, Turks, and the French occupied it. That is more than four thousand years of outside control! Today the struggle continues as the Shia Hezbollah opposition militia-party, sponsored by Syria and Iran, vies for dominance over the democratically elected coalition government of Christians, Sunnis, and Druze. Until I broke away from abuse in my early twenties, my life was just like the history of Lebanon: controlled by someone else.

Lebanon is like a kaleidoscope. With each turn of history the picture of the country changes. Like fragments of broken glass, the diverse people of Lebanon tumble around within the boundaries of their tiny nation vying for new positions and more power. In time, as the picture changes, certain religious or political groups become more dominant while opposing groups lose control, all the while affirming their identity and their role in the state. The one stable fact about Lebanon today is its instability. It continues to undergo kaleidoscopic change.

My mother, who was named Samiyah, was born in Beirut a few years after the French Mandate was implemented. Her father's name was Hassan, and her mother was called Soraya. They were both Arab Lebanese and Shia Muslims. Hassan was well known and highly regarded as the mayor of his mountainous village. The date of my mother's birth has been a family debate for as long as I can remember, because she has no birth certificate. It was common in the old country not to have a written document as proof of birth. Births were dated sometimes by the seasons, by some event such as a late winter snow or flood, by a crisis in the family, or some other memory hook. As long as the family remembered the approximate date, it was enough.

My father was named Waleed. He was born in Highland Park, Michigan. His father, Ali, was of Lebanese and Italian descent. His mother, Valentina, was French. She was Jewish. She had three sons. When my father was very young, probably five or six years old, his mother disappeared under the mysterious circumstances mentioned in the previous chapter. He was sent to live with relatives on a farm in Lebanon, as Ali was a playboy and was not responsible enough to raise his sons. Much of my father's childhood was lived in foster homes, and then, as a young adult, he lived in Paris, France. When he became of age, he enlisted in the French Navy.

My father met my mother during military leave in Beirut and wanted to marry her, but she was already promised to her cousin. Arranged marriage was a common practice in Lebanon and throughout the Middle East in those days and still is. Girls typically do not have any choice in the matter unless they obstinately refuse as I did. Then all hell breaks loose. Anyway, following her heart, my mother eloped with my father. Her family immediately ostracized the new couple because they broke with tradition, but eventually everyone forgave them, and their marriage was accepted.

My mother was twenty-two years old when I was born, and my father was thirty. I was not their first child. My mother had given birth to a boy, but he was stillborn. When I was born, the spring rains came after a long drought. The family believed this was a good omen. They believed that I was special. Like the refreshing rains, I brought new life to the family. I was delivered by a midwife, a family member, as is customary in Arab villages. Unlike my mother, I do have a birth certificate. It is written in Arabic and French.

Women in my parents' generation often did not receive an education in the old country. Girls were not encouraged to go to school because they might become worldly, get seduced into giving up their virginity, or, God forbid, marry someone without parental approval. A girl with an education might be impossible to control. In my experience, boys always had privileged status. Although I grew up in America, I was raised with old country ideas.

My mother brought me to the United States when I was two years old. Moving to America was both frightening and exciting to her. It was an adventure into unknown territory and an entirely new life, but leaving Lebanon also filled her with sorrow. Leaving her father, mother, and siblings was devastating. It was something she would never forget, and she would come to regret it. In later years, she even blamed herself for her father's death. She thought that if she had not left the old country, her father would still be living. She was close to her father. He loved her and favored her.

That was not the case with either my father or my grandfather and me. The sexual molestation I experienced at the hands of my grandfather and the physical abuse inflicted by my father had a kaleidoscopic effect upon me. Other abusers added to the effect until I finally began to control my own destiny. Until then, no matter how the years turned, my life had the same old aspects of abuse: different situations, different abusers, different times, different places, but always abuse. Abusers attempt to dominate their victims, to turn them into whatever picture they want to create. Abuse is all about control.

Breakaway

The sky lifts not, we push our way
Inch by inch through stubborn clay,
Until we feel within our hearts
A growing inspiration.

God Bless the U.S.A.

MERICA, AMERICA, LAND OF FREEDOM AND hope! My father had already returned to America several months before my mother and I boarded the plane in Beirut for the flight to New York. Like millions of other immigrants, the sadness my mother felt for the old country was overcome by the enthusiasm she felt for America. Possibilities not even dreamed of in the old country were just a few hours away. A new husband, a new baby, a new country, a new life! What could be better than that?

I love New York. I wish my parents had stayed there. I love museums. I love the theatre. I love great music and great food. I love cosmopolitan life. New York has everything, but it did not have the work my father needed at the time, so he had gone right on to Dearborn, Michigan, to find the job he stayed at for thirty years. Mother and I spent only one night in New York before we flew on to Dearborn.

Dearborn is synonymous with the Ford Motor Company. It is the hometown of Henry Ford and the *Dearborn Independent* where for several years he published his hatred of Zionism and Jews in general. It is also the home of Ford's headquarters and the famous Rouge Plant where my father worked along with thousands of others on the assembly lines.

There were blacks in the factory in those days, but not many. They could live in Detroit but they were not welcome to live in Dearborn. They were allowed only to work or to shop there before the Civil Rights Movement of the 1960s. Of course, in Mayor Hubbard's history we are told that blacks (he used the N-word) were as equal as anyone else in Dearborn, but I never saw a black child in my school, not one, starting with kindergarten and continuing into high school. The reality of white supremacy in Dearborn in those days can be summarized by what George Orwell wrote in *Animal Farm*: "All animals are equal but some are more equal than others."

So I was transplanted from the diverse cultural soil of Lebanon to a simmering pot of prejudice in Dearborn, Michigan. Change came in the 1960s. That is when Detroit was set on fire. I lived through the Detroit riots in the summer of 1967, so I experienced firsthand the beginnings of change.

I was very much a racist in those days. That is what I learned from my culture. All blacks were inferior and were to be shunned or feared. All whites except those who spoke Arabic were hillbillies. They were also to be avoided but less so than blacks. The racism and prejudice that characterized Dearborn had a profound effect on me. It isolated my family from the non-Arab community and became a major part of why I would receive so many beatings as a teenager. Dearborn's intolerance contrasted sharply with hopes and dreams of equal opportunity in America.

Fortunately, time has brought enlightenment to Dearborn. I have a niece who is married to a wonderful black man. They broke the color barrier. They were shunned as a couple at first, but the family came to love him over time. Now they have children, and they are all welcome in the family. It took several years and a lot of forbearance and persistence on the part of my niece. Intermarriage was out of the question when I was growing up. The roots of prejudice are difficult to eradicate.

It was not until my third marriage in 1984 that I began to realize how wrong and unfair prejudice is. It took a long time and a lot of love and patience on my husband's part to get me through the stubborn clay of prejudice. He was my inspiration. Now I love everyone and fight for fairness and equal rights. It seems like it should be easy to change one's opinions about people, but it is not. It is hard work. It is so hard that when you do change, you may find it difficult to love and accept people who will not change. If you have never seen the light of fairness and equality, you have no idea what it is.

My father was not an affectionate man, but for everything he was not, he was a good provider. He never missed a day's work at the Ford Motor Company. He always walked to work, even when it was raining, snowing and blowing, or bitter cold. He wanted to avoid using his car. He was very frugal. He dreamed the American dream: to drive a new car and to own a house.

When we first came to America, my parents lived in a basement apartment owned by another Lebanese couple. It was not a pleasant place, and very soon they looked for other housing. They found an apartment on Dix Avenue and stayed there for a couple of years before they were finally able to buy a house on Ferney Street. The house on Ferney Street is the only place I remember living as a child. There was a big back yard where my father planted fruit trees of various kinds to help with the grocery bill. We also had a huge garden. We never went hungry.

My mother was not employed outside the home in the early years. She stayed home having babies, one after another. She was also in charge of the money, and she saved and saved. My parents paid cash for everything but their home: no credit, no loans, just cash for all purchases. There were lean times, of course, but they never depended on welfare or state subsidies. They believed in hard work and living within their means. In less than five years they had their mortgage paid for free and clear. The house had only one story, and it was small. The family was growing rapidly as a baby arrived almost every year. They had to do something, so they remodeled the entire house and added a second story to it.

My mother liked to have the latest styles in furniture and interior design. People always laugh when I tell them that she never took the plastic off the living room furniture! We kids were never allowed in the living room anyway. It was off limits. Only special guests were entertained there. All in all, my mother was happy with her new surroundings. She had many Middle Eastern as well as American friends. She has a great out-going personality.

Some of her friends had basements equipped with kitchens, bathrooms, bedrooms, and shared laundry rooms. My parents loved the idea and built a basement apartment to rent out by the week, a common practice at the time. They rented it out to young families, some of whom stayed longer than a year and became like part of our family. I remember Tibby from Virginia, Vernell from North Carolina, and Sherry from India. These women were just getting started in life and did the best they could to raise their children and love their husbands. They were all wonderful women. They all had dreams. Like them, I became a dreamer.

We wait and wait until it's time
To germinate, to grow, to climb,
To leave behind our shuttered state
For another orientation.

Dream Girl

FREEDOM FROM ABUSE IS NOT EASILY WON. IT IS a very complex and long process. I dreamed of freedom every day of my young life. I prayed for it and cried for it. Away from home, I saw others who enjoyed liberty, but there was no freedom at home for me.

A life of abuse is like a box with many compartments. When the abuse is going on, you do everything you can to sort things out and make some order out of life. You are conscious of it all. But when the abuse is over, you sometimes seal up some of the compartments. Psychologists call this suppression when you do it consciously and repression when it is done unconsciously.

When I was in my late thirties, another niece pulled me aside and nervously told me about the sexual abuse she had been through as a child and still had to endure as a young teenager. Although her situation was different than mine (she was forced to have oral sex with her uncle), the emotional wounds were just as deep. She remained silent about it until she was seventeen years old. Fed up with it and not knowing what to do, she came to me for help. She was brave to talk about it. She told me the whole story because she trusted me. She also knew that I had been abused as a child, but she was not aware of what happened to me in my grandfather's room. Neither was I. Her experience triggered memories that had been repressed.

The floodgates opened and the reservoir of pain and suffering that I had stored up for over thirty years came gushing out. I suddenly became conscious of what my grandfather had done to me, and I did not know how to deal with it. It was a giant, grizzly bear that came roaring to life after many years of hibernation to devour my peace of mind. I had no defense against it. I sought professional help. It was a long and difficult battle, but I eventually tamed the bear and became stronger through the struggle.

I did not have the privilege of counseling as a child. I had to make it on my own. I could not tell anyone about my grandfather's room. The machete silenced me. Fear is a great motivator to an innocent child. It was impossible to escape my grandfather's torture as long as it was going on, but when he stopped, I locked the door to his room in my mind and escaped from it. That is when I became a dream girl.

In retrospect, I began my acting career at the age of eight. I learned to play two roles: Little Mother and Dream Girl. As Little Mother, I shared the responsibility of raising my siblings. My parents' fertility became my curse.

The curse was an ancient one that still persists in my culture. I was born a female. Females have second-class status in my culture. It is written in the sacred books, and it is written on the hearts of men. Arab men put a great deal of stock in having a son to carry on their name. It has been that way for all of recorded history. It is a disgrace not to have a son. Sons receive a greater portion of the inheritance: they get the house, the money, the jewels, whatever, and it is up to them if they want to share it with female siblings. Females are at the mercy of males, pure and simple.

Females are born to serve. I was a certified servant. Most obviously, men do not do housework. That domain belongs exclusively to the female gender. Boys and men do not help.

Being persona non grata in a male-dominated culture has many drawbacks, especially if you happen to be the firstborn female. My role as Little Mother became increasingly dominant as the years passed and each of my siblings was born. I was made to help carry the load for cooking, cleaning, and caregiving.

My servant status kicked into high gear when I was about eight years old. From that time forward, I helped my mother cook breakfast, lunch, and dinner when I was not in school. During the school year, I still had to help with making breakfast and then was responsible to clean up before going off to school. I always looked forward to school. Of course, my household duties often made me late, so I walked alone to school most days. Cooking chores awaited me when I returned home as well, and the dinner dishes had to be done.

Cleaning was also an endless task. Scrubbing the kitchen and bathroom floors was to be done by hand, on my knees with a scrub brush. My mother purchased the brushes from the Fuller brush man who sold them door-to-door. The use of a mop was not allowed, as it was thought to be less effective.

Washing clothes was really hard work. Our machine did not have a rinse and spin cycle like the modern washers. Rinsing was a separate process. Once the clothes were washed in the machine, they had to be taken out by hand, put into a tub of clean rinse water with bluing added to brighten the clothes, and then put through the wringer. The wringer was comprised of two rollers under spring tension attached to the top of the washing machine. It had a crank on the right-hand side. Each piece of clothing had to be put through the wringer separately. I put the clothes through the wringer with my left hand and turned the crank with my right. The wet clothes were very heavy, and my arm frequently got caught in the wringer. The clothes went into a basket on a table. The water extracted from the clothes drained back into the tub. I was so small I had to stand on a chair to do this job. It was hard work.

Breakaway

Once rinsed and wrung out, the wet clothes were carried out to the lines in the yard for drying. Hanging clothes outside was not easy either, since I was too small to reach the clothesline. I had to use a chair, stepping up and down to hang the clothes on the line, one piece at a time. My mother had to help me with the big pieces like sheets and bath towels. The work was demanding for her as well, since she was pregnant much of the time. When the clothes were dry, I had to take them down carefully so as not to get them dirty, up and down on the chair again, one piece at a time. Finally, everything had to be folded. To this day, with all the conveniences we have for doing laundry, I truly hate the job, especially the folding part.

Caregiving was also never-ending. Early on, I learned to change diapers and tend to the other care and feeding needs of my siblings. As the children got older, my responsibilities grew as well. Whatever personal desires I had were not considered. I could attend to my own needs, like homework, only when my chores were done.

I also sacrificed in other areas. For example, I never had a birthday party or a toy. I was told that I was the oldest, and I should not expect to have playthings. I was too big. That was true whether I was five, ten, or in my teens. The other children could enjoy such amenities, but not me. I was Little Mother. I turned to my dreams for relief.

As Dream Girl, I had two escapes. My first escape was music. As soon as Elvis Presley arrived on the scene, he immediately became my thrill as he was for so many millions of girls. I was never a screamer like other girls, but I was wowed by his looks, and I listened to his songs over and over again. Elvis topped the charts in 1956 with *Heartbreak Hotel*, *Don't Be Cruel*, *Hound Dog*, *Love Me Tender*, and *I Want You, I Need You, I Love You*. I still remember most of the lyrics of his songs. I dreamed of seeing him one day. Years later I attended three of Elvis' concerts and even sneaked a 8mm movie camera under my coat into one of them. I still have the film, but Elvis looks like a white dot on a black screen!

Breakaway

It was a thrill to go to the King's concert on September 29, 1974. I was given free tickets for the upcoming show on October 4 with front row seats for three, so I took two of my friends. Elvis was only a few feet away from us. It was unbelievable! I met his backup singers, the *Jordanaires* and the *Sweet Inspirations,* as well as the band members and others on his support team when I was invited to his private party at the Pontchartrain Hotel in downtown Detroit. My childhood dream came true!

Elvis topped the charts again in 1957 with *All Shook Up, Jailhouse Rock, Let Me Be Your Teddy Bear* and *Too Much.* Of course, there were other artists I liked besides Elvis. Some of my favorites were the Everly Brothers (*All I Have To Do Is Dream; Bye, Bye Love*), Ricky Nelson (*Poor Little Fool*), the Silhouettes (*Get A Job*), Bobby Darin (*Mack The Knife*), and the Canadian-born, Lebanese singer Paul Anka (*Diana, Lonely Boy, Puppy Love,* and *Put Your Head On My Shoulder*). In fact, it would be hard to find a song on the charts from 1956 to 1960 that I did not like. I was all rock and roll.

My other escape was dancing. I have always loved to dance. Sometimes my girlfriends and I would dance to rock and roll tunes during recess at school. There was also a park not too far from my house where I would go and listen to music and dance with friends. We twisted, strolled, and did the mashed potato whenever we could.

I bought 45 rpm records of my favorite hits and won more records in city-sponsored dance contests at the park in our neighborhood. Whenever I could sneak a moment for myself at home, I would lock myself in the bedroom and play my records. Although I did not have many, they were my prized possessions, something that belonged only to me. I played them over and over again. I still have a small collection of them.

My life was also enhanced by the new transistor radio. Because my time was not my own, I relished the opportunity to listen to my transistor. Only AM stations were available at the time, but that was good enough for me. My radio was pocket-sized and had a single earpiece. I usually put the earpiece in my ear and danced alone in my room. The quality was not very good, but I learned that it was better if I put the radio right up to my ear rather than using the earpiece. That is how I listened most of the time, but it was a little hard to dance that way. When I tired of dancing, I put the radio on the pillow next to my ear and listened until I was ready to go to sleep. What a great escape that was!

The mind is wonderful at making ways to escape. Beginning at the age of eight, my mind became a magic carpet that carried me far away from the realities of my daily life. It took me from Little Mother to Dream Girl. I never stopped dreaming.

Breakaway

Our heads held high, our hearts intact,
We break the ground in one proud act,
And sense the warmth upon our pates
From Sol's illumination.

Sentenced

FROM THE BEGINNING I WAS NOT IN CONTROL OF my life. I had to do whatever I was told to do. This was very hard for me, since I had my own free (and some would say stubborn) will. I wanted to choose my life and do what I wanted to do, but that was not to be. As often as I played Dream Girl, I could not escape the role of Little Mother. Then my life changed.

I was almost thirteen years old and just developing enough to wear a beginner's bra when I started to menstruate. It was terrifying. It happened while I was at school. No one told me about menstruation, so I did not know what to expect. I was on my way to the girl's lavatory when I noticed that I was bleeding. I screamed and ran to the restroom in tears. My friend, Teresa, was already there.

"What's wrong, Nadia? What's wrong?"

"I'm bleeding to death. I'm dying," I cried. The cramps were killing me.

Teresa laughed and said, "You're not dying. You're just having your period. All girls start their period. Here, wear this."

She handed me a thick, white block of cotton called a Kotex pad. It was so thick and huge it felt like a mattress between my legs all day long. I felt like everyone in school was watching me walk funny. When I got home, I did not tell anyone about my period. I was too embarrassed. But my mother found out anyway a few days later when she reached her next cycle. I took her pads without telling her and used up the whole box. She confronted me, and I confessed, "Yes, I've had my first period."

When my teacher heard about my change, she gave me a little booklet to help me understand what causes the menstrual cycle and how it relates to fertility and pregnancy. I took it home and showed it to my mother. She went into orbit. She could not read or write (remember no school for girls in the old country when she was there), but the pictures were clear enough.

"Who gave you this booklet? I'm going to the school tomorrow to talk with the principal," she screamed in Arabic.

There was nothing in the booklet about actual sexual relations, but it had graphic illustrations of the vagina, clitoris, and ovaries—the whole deal. That is what made my mother mad. She could not believe what the school was teaching me. She took the booklet away from me and tore it to pieces.

As I said, I loved school because there no one told me what to do: clean this, clean that, hang this, hang that, scrub this, scrub that. If I wanted to read a book, I could go to the study hall where it was almost always quiet. Reading at home was not possible. Too many distractions kept me from studying. My siblings were always yelling, or my parents watched their favorite programs on the black and white TV with the volume so loud it was impossible to concentrate. It was always noisy at our house. I liked to go to the public library to read.

My father did not always believe me when I told him I was going to the library. I always had to tell him when I went, but I did not tell him that sometimes I met my friends there so we could do our homework together. I was not allowed to have American girlfriends. "They're a bad influence," my parents would tell me. "They have boyfriends. They have sex. They get pregnant. They're not your friends. They don't care about you." I could have only Arabic friends. I knew Arab girls, but I did not hang out with them. They were restricted, too. Of course, I could not have male friends under any circumstances.

My father often came to the library to check on me to see if I was alone. One day, he surprised me. He came to the library and saw me studying with my friends. He quietly came and grabbed me by the hair and proceeded to drag me out to the car. It was so embarrassing to be dragged through the library and across the yard in front of all of my classmates. He drove the few blocks to our house in a rage. Before he stopped the car, I was already out the door and running up to my room, crying all the way. I knew what was coming.

"What's wrong?" my mother asked.

"Baba's going to beat me," I cried hysterically. "He found me at the library with my friends. I didn't do anything wrong. I was just reading and doing my homework."

My father was downstairs looking for the belt he routinely used on me. Having found it, he ran up the stairs, flew into my bedroom, and began lashing me with the belt.

"Please, Baba, don't hurt me," I cried. "Please, don't hurt me. I didn't do anything. Please, Baba! Please!" I broke free and ran downstairs with him chasing me. He caught me and threw me down on the floor, kicking me all over my body and banging my head on the wall. My father was not a big man. He was only about five feet eight, but he was very strong, and I was small-boned and petite. I could not resist him. I just kept screaming for him to stop but he would not listen. He continued with the beating, yelling at me the whole time.

"How many times have I told you not to go with American kids? You'll get a bad reputation. People will talk. How many times? How many times?" Finally, he stopped and left me lying on the floor. The welts and bruises would remain for days, but worse than the beating was the way he walked away when he finished. It was routine. He would look at me in disgust, turn on his heel, and leave me lying on the floor like a pile of dirt.

From then on, I came home from school and did not stop at the library. I had to study at home where I could be seen, as from that day forward my father never trusted me again.

Months passed and I grew very depressed. I was going on fourteen, and my life was getting worse. I hated it. I longed to be eighteen so I could leave home and live on my own. I wanted freedom more than life itself. I wanted to be like American boys and girls: free to walk home with friends, free to go to a movie, free to go to the school dances. I wanted to go to recreation night where students played ping-pong, basketball, or badminton. I wanted to enjoy just one night of sports and fun with other students. I was never allowed to go. I was trapped in my culture.

I was a normal, fun-loving, friendly girl who had reached the age of puberty. But, because I was a Lebanese girl in Dearborn, I experienced a whole new meaning of the term *period*. I was taught in school that a period ended a sentence, a complete and independent thought. But for me, a *period*—the menstrual period— was the *beginning* of a sentence, a sentence of bondage and abuse. It served to restrict my movements and isolate me from my friends. My passage into womanhood gave my parents another reason to control me. They feared I would get pregnant. So independence was only a dream for me as I passed from a stolen childhood to the trials of life as a teenager.

Part Two

Teenage Trials

Breakaway

Darkness now behind us lies.
We lift our hands to vaulted skies
And drink the air into our lungs
In sudden transformation.

Secrets

MY FOURTEENTH BIRTHDAY WAS LIKE EVERY other. There was no celebration—no party. I was too busy. My mother had already given birth to seven children and was exhausted. Feeling trapped, she took a job at the Pontchartrain Hotel, dishing off to me more of the responsibility for taking care of all of my siblings. They got bigger. The lunches got bigger. The pile of dirty clothes got bigger, and I seemed to be the one that everyone leaned on to get the job done. School was the only escape from the drudgery of my life.

One day, I was walking to school when I noticed a cute teenage boy dressed in blue jeans and a tan pullover shirt. He was sitting on his front porch as I walked by. He saw me and whistled. When I stopped and looked, he very shyly said, "Hi." Flushed and nervous, I quickly said "Hi," too, and kept walking. It took all my strength not to turn my head and look back. I wondered who this boy was. He was new in the neighborhood. I had never seen him at school. He was all I could think about that day. I could not wait to go home, hoping to see him again. I liked the way he looked. I wanted to meet him. I had a lot of questions to ask him. My curiosity was definitely piqued.

School was finally out. I walked home with my best friend, Teresa. She was a Mexican girl who was born in Gary, Indiana. Her father moved their family to Dearborn where the Ford Motor Company employed him. Most of the men in Dearborn worked at the Rouge Plant. Teresa and I met in the fifth grade. We did not like each other at first, but very soon we became best friends. Teresa was dark complexioned and had straight, thick, black hair. She was very quiet and very shy. We shared all of our secrets with each other, many of which we would keep to ourselves for years to come. I could not wait to tell her my new secret.

I told Teresa about the boy as soon as we were alone. I told her how cute he was and how shy. She wanted me to show her where he lived. We were excited as we approached his house. There he was sitting on his front porch. I waved and he waved back. Teresa continued walking on Wyoming Street to go home, and I turned onto Williams Street. I was walking at the side of his house when he suddenly appeared on the back porch. He sat on the steps and called out to me.

"What's your name?" He spoke slowly with a southern drawl.

I stopped and said, "Nadia, what's yours?"

"I'm Billy, come and sit by me," he said. I was so nervous that I just giggled and ran home, happy that I had met the best-looking boy in Dearborn. Billy had blue eyes and the most beautiful black lashes I had ever seen on a boy. He was about five feet five and looked like a smaller version of Elvis. He was from Tennessee, not far from Memphis. He was fourteen years old. Meeting Billy brought some sunshine into my life, but I had to keep him a secret since I was not allowed to have boyfriends. I knew that my father would beat me if he discovered I was talking to an American boy.

I saw Billy at school and walked home with him as often as possible, and Billy would sometimes walk in front my house hoping to see me. When he did, I got scared. I immediately ran up the stairs and opened my bedroom window and quietly told him to leave. I feared we would get caught. Still, not allowed to date or have American friends, I determined to do what I wanted to do, and I definitely wanted to get to know Billy. I decided to suffer the beatings from my father that I knew would come if he saw me with Billy. I looked forward to my eighteenth birthday so I could be free to leave home, and I believed I could survive the beatings until then, not knowing at the time that it would almost cost me my life. Of course, I did not have sex with Billy or any other boy. I was a virgin. I was constantly told that if I allowed a boy to kiss me I would get pregnant.

Then sure enough, it happened. One day, I secretly met Billy in the lobby of the Wyoming Hotel across the street from where my grandfather had a room at the Dix Hotel. We sat on the steps inside and talked. Billy leaned over and sneaked a kiss, and I almost had a heart attack. I screamed at him, cursed him, and told him that my father was going to kill me.

"Why, because I kissed you?" he asked.

Sobbing, I answered, "I'm going to get pregnant! My father said that I'd get pregnant if a boy kissed me."

Billy laughed and said confidently, "That's not how a girl gets pregnant. Don't you know about sex?"

"No, what about it?" I was so naïve.

My sex education tutorial was about to begin when I noticed my brother and two sisters walking past the grocery store at the corner. I knew they were looking for me. My father had sent out his spies so they could tattle on me. I waited for them to turn the corner and immediately opened the door and ran out, leaving Billy stunned on the steps.

I ran all the way home. I pretended to be unaware of the search that was going on for me. I could not make a move without someone squealing on me. The little spies were out every day in full force. My father threatened to beat them if they did not tattle.

Needless to say, they always did his bidding. No matter how hard I tried to get them on my side, they still tattled. My siblings were well trained to go against me and tell all that they saw and heard.

I did not care. I was determined not to let my parents control my life. The more they controlled, the more I resisted. I needed to be social. I was going to do whatever I wanted, everything except have sex. If I walked home from school with American friends, my father, informed by the spies, would be waiting for me with belt in hand. He could not believe that I would go back and do the very same thing that caused me to be beaten before. After being thrashed with the belt, punched, knocked to the floor, and stomped on, I would get up, storm out the door, and return to my friends. Seeing me hurt and crying, they always consoled me and wished they could do something to help me, but what could they do?

One day after school, my friends and I stopped at the corner soda shop. Teresa and her boyfriend, Brian, an Irish girlfriend named Karen, and Donna, a southern girlfriend, were there with me. We were sitting at the counter, drinking Cream Soda (my favorite) and listening to the jukebox, when Billy walked in. I could not believe it. We sat at the counter and had a soda together. Then I stepped down from the stool, went over to the jukebox, dropped a nickel in, and played my favorite song by the Chiffons: *One Fine Day*. And what a fine day it was! After my record stopped playing, Billy played *Hey, Paula* for me. It almost made me want to change my name!

Time flew. Soon, Billy and I had known each other for almost a year. The kids at school all knew Billy and I were going steady. Teresa and Brian were going steady, too. Teresa had total freedom. She was allowed to have parties with friends at her house. She could discuss anything with her mother: sex, boys, anything. My mother wanted me silenced whenever I asked questions. Every question was taboo at my house. I always wished that I could have a life of freedom and love at home, but it never happened.

Breakaway

Billy and I were content to see each other only at school and occasionally to walk home together with our friends. The distance from school was not all that far, but it took a while with Billy. He walked sort of like James Dean with a really slow stroll. Not that it bothered me, because I was happy to be with him, especially since all the girls in my class thought he was good-looking.

It turned out that Billy's good looks were a veneer on a flawed character. I thought he was committed to me, but I soon discovered that he had other interests in the neighborhood. I happened to be on my way to the corner store one day when I saw him coming out of a nearby apartment building with a girl. She was not someone I knew. I had never seen her at school. What was Billy doing with her? He saw me and quickly motioned for her to go back inside. He looked very guilty as he strolled over to me.

"Hi, Billy, what's going on? Who's that girl?" I asked with a sharp tone in my voice.

"She's just a friend. We were watching TV together," he replied nervously.

"What's her name?"

"Kathy, she's just a friend."

"Really, Billy?" I said sarcastically. "You were just watching TV with Kathy. How nice. Well, I don't have time for you right now, Billy, but we need to talk. Maybe I'll see you tomorrow. And then again, maybe I won't."

Of course, I smelled a rat. Why did she run back inside if she were just a friend? I knew there was more to the story, but I wanted to plan my response instead of arguing on the spot. I had a sinking feeling that Billy was keeping his own secrets. Already, I was learning to trust my intuition, to listen to my heart.

There would be a lot more rats to smell before I was through with Billy.

Although constrained against our will,
Our buried dreams define us still.
With diligence we stay our course
Without a reservation.

The Proposal

VERY SOON AFTER MY FIFTEENTH BIRTHDAY, I was given an airline ticket on a Pan Am flight to Beirut, Lebanon. My sister went with me. I was being sent there against my will to marry a cousin whom I had never met. I knew that he was much older than I was, but that is all I was told. My marriage to him would give him United States citizenship. I was to become a means for him to emigrate, a human passport. However, my family did not know that my aunt Grace had secretly advised me not to go through with the marriage. "If you do, Nadia," she said, "you'll never see the United States again." Her words were on my mind as I boarded the plane. What was I to do?

It was my first time in a jet. As we were flying above the clouds, I found myself looking for God. I stayed up most of the night looking out the window, hoping to see God's face. I finally fell asleep looking for him. I woke to a brilliant sunrise somewhere over France.

Breakaway

Presently, a voice came over the intercom telling us to fasten our seatbelts as we were descending to refuel. I was thrilled to land in Paris, the City of Light famous for its Eiffel Tower and the River Seine. I knew that my father had lived in Paris and that my grandmother was of French heritage. I also knew the names of some famous people who had lived in Paris like Picasso and Brigitte Bardot. I wondered what life might be like for me if I lived in Paris. Would I be famous, too?

While the plane was being prepared for the final leg of our journey, my sister and I had lunch at the airport. The menu, of course, was in French, and since we could not read it, ordering was an adventure. We managed somehow. The layover was short, and soon we had to hurry to the departure gate. We boarded with the help of flight attendants who thankfully spoke English.

After a short time in the air, the landscape of France gave way to the Mediterranean Sea. The colors of the Mediterranean were the most amazing blues I could have imagined. Shades of turquoise along the coast framed the rich, royal blues of the deeper waters farther offshore. I shall never forget the first time I saw the Mediterranean Sea.

The flight from Paris to Beirut took almost six hours, counting one hour for the time change. My heart leaped with excitement as the breakers of the Mediterranean touched the white sands of the beach in Beirut. Not only had I never seen such a magnificent and large body of water, I had never seen a beach! I was so mesmerized! It took my mind off the reason why I was being sent to the old country.

Several members of my mother's family greeted us at the arrival gate. They were so happy to see us. They took us to the home of my uncle Hassan, the youngest of my mother's brothers. He was so handsome and so kind. He welcomed us with a big hug and made us feel at home. The women prepared a welcome feast for us in the Lebanese tradition. We ate too much, visited a long time, and, exhausted from the long flight and jet lag, finally went to bed. The fun part of the trip was over.

The next day, one family after another arrived early to greet my sister and me and to invite us into their homes later. Everyone was excited about the marriage proposal ceremony. Celebration was in the air. By mid-morning the crowd had swelled to about fifty people. I had no idea how large my mother's family was.

The women immediately put themselves to work. They loaded tables with *pita, falafel, kibbe, tabouli, hummus, kafta, shish kebab, shawarma, fattoush,* and, of course, plenty of *baklava* in various shapes and sizes. There is nothing like Lebanese food and hospitality, and this was all being done for me! It was a spread fit for a queen.

After lunch, the men took chairs out to the terrace and set them up in a semicircle. It was a warm and sunny day. As the guests took their seats, I was given a chair facing them. I enjoyed the attention, but there was a smoldering volcano in the pit of my stomach. I was very nervous and began to feel hot and sweaty. I was the main act, and the show was about to begin.

Of course, the groom's family was there as well, seated conspicuously in the front row where they could inspect me. The groom was about five feet eight with dark hair and dark eyes shielded by a single eyebrow. He was standing at the back of the audience with a big smile on his face. I had no idea whether he was a good man or not, but he was certainly not my type.

When everyone was assembled, Uncle Hassan stood up to announce that the marriage ceremony was to take place the following week. He spoke for a few minutes, mostly about what a nice girl I was and how happy my parents were that I was being married in the old country. When he finished, everyone waited breathlessly for my response. They did not have long to wait.

Uncle Hassan turned to me and said, "Nadia, *habibti,* let's hear what you have to say. Are you happy about taking Assam as your husband?"

My reply sent a shock wave through the crowd. *"Absolutely not! No! Uncle Hassan, I won't marry him!"* I turned and pointed to the formerly grinning groom. His face now resembled a stone blowfish. His eyes were wide with amazement and his mouth was frozen open. The stunned spectators could do nothing but stare at me. No one moved a muscle. I tried to remain calm, but suddenly the rumbling volcano in my stomach erupted. I bolted for the bathroom and locked the door.

While I was dealing with my volcano, there was another violent movement outside. I had created a riot, but I did not care. I was too busy with the flow of lava. I lost my share of the lovely banquet, and before I had time to regain my composure, Uncle Hassan's wife launched herself at the bathroom door and demanded, "*Come out of there, Nadia! Come out right now!*"

I came out all right, looking a very pale shade of green and feeling faint. Nevertheless, the business at hand had to be dealt with. Aunt Fatima ushered me back to the expectant crowd and stood beside me with her hand on my shoulder, as I slumped into my chair.

"What do you mean, no?" everyone asked in chorus. Unless you've seen an excited group of Arabs, especially Arab women, you have no idea what that scene was like.

"No, means no, just no. I won't marry him!" I pointed to the blowfish again for emphasis. "I want to go back home to the States."

The crowd went silent again. Then the humiliated groom started yelling obscenities and invoking curses on me in Arabic. Arabic is a wonderful language for cursing. He put on a magnificent performance that pretty well ended the whole show. He disappeared stage right, still swearing oaths against the day I was born. The show was over. I held the stage. The audience did not know what to do. Naturally, there was no applause. Nobody moved. Time stood still.

Then instantly, like a Rocky Mountain cloudburst, there was a flurry of activity as the frenzied women came to life. They surrounded me and carried on in the most marvelous display of screaming and cursing you can imagine. It was pretty obvious that none of the women were going to support my cause. Frankly, I began to be concerned for my safety. The ladies were getting out of control. Ironically, I felt that most of the men were either amused or even possibly on my side. At least, judging by their laughter, they seemed to fully enjoy the manner in which the former groom departed. However, none of them spoke up in my defense, perhaps out of fear of facing their women folk when they returned home. In any event, I waited like Joan of Arc for my fate to be determined, expecting to be burned at the stake or worse.

As it turned out, the stake might have been more pleasant. After a heated debate, it was decided that I should be put under house arrest and restricted from going anywhere alone. Everyone hoped that I would change my mind given some time. Two male cousins were appointed as bodyguards to accompany me whenever I was granted a few hours of freedom from my assigned prison. Unless I had a change of heart, I would eventually be sent to the mountains to live in isolation with my eighty-year-old grandmother. In the meantime, as a holding measure, I was to stay in Uncle Hassan's house, literally, quarantined from people like a leper and restricted from sightseeing or anything else that might remotely be described as fun or interesting to a teenager.

After several months of house arrest with Uncle Hassan, daily monitored by the two aforementioned bodyguards, the prisoner was transported to the mountains where my grandmother dutifully assumed her role as warden. There was no possibility of escape, since the whole mountain seemed to have been put on notice to monitor my movements. I was allowed to take walks on the mountain, escorted of course, where I could look down on the city of Beirut and its environs. These outings always earned glares and sneers from neighbors who knew that I had broken with tradition. I contemplated daily how I could escape and get back to America. How?

Weeks and months passed with no change in my situation. My spirit grew dark, as I lost hope. I sank deeper into depression with each passing day. There seemed to be no way out for me. Desperate and determined to be released after almost a year of house arrest, it occurred to me that I should write a letter to my parents. It was not a long letter. I simply had to make my point. I wrote something like this:

Breakaway

Dear Mama and Baba,

> *I'm in prison here. I didn't do anything wrong. I just refused to marry Assam. I will not marry him or anyone else here. If you don't send me a ticket within two weeks to return to the States, I'm going to jump off the mountain and kill myself.*

Nadia

I sincerely meant it. I wrote the letter and managed to secretly mail it. The response came quicker than I expected. My parents sent the tickets along with my letter to Uncle Hassan. Naturally, the natives were upset that the prisoner had managed to notify the outside world without the warden's knowledge. That is putting it mildly. They were furious, disgraced, humiliated, shamed, and a hundred other things too unpleasant to talk about. Uncle Hassan, God bless him, seemed to be the only rational person in the bunch, but he was still taking the side of my mother and the rest of the family when he arrived to take me off the mountain.

"Why are you doing this to your family, Nadia?" he demanded.

"Because it's not right, Uncle Hassan. I'm still only fifteen years old. I don't want to get married and have babies like all the other Arab girls. No matter how long you lock me up, I'm not going to marry anyone."

"You've wasted your parent's money, *habibti*. Why didn't you tell them you weren't going to marry Assam?" Uncle Hassan sounded sincere, but I sensed that he already knew the answer.

"I did tell them, Uncle, but they wouldn't listen. They thought that once I came here and stayed for a while I'd change my mind."

"And you won't change your mind?"

"No way. Never. I'm sorry, but I've wasted a year of my life here already. I'm behind in school. I have no friends. I have no life. I want to go home. Please Uncle, let me go home."

I made my case. Uncle Hassan seemed to understand. He did not argue with me. He was a good man with a big heart.

A week later, my sister and I were back in America.

Thank you, and God bless you, Aunt Grace!

Our roots remain secure and sound
Beneath the surface of the ground,
While we must chart in this new world
A course of navigation.

It's Not My Party

I WAS ALMOST SIXTEEN, LOOKING FORWARD TO another birthday and being one year closer to independence. My life was devoid of happiness. I wished that I had somewhere to run to, somewhere to hide, but there was nowhere to go. I did not have the courage to run away and try to live on my own. I was still a certified introvert who was sheltered, timid, and shy. My self-esteem was near zero. I had no confidence that I could succeed in anything. No matter how good my grades in school were, no matter that I was on the honor roll most times, no matter how many spelling bees I won, at home I was nobody. The many times that my father called me names as he pounded my head on the floor, kicked me with his shoes, or slammed me against the wall, took their toll. I felt that I was ugly, skinny, and stupid.

As I approached sixteen, life went on as usual except that my parents stepped up the effort to marry me off to an Arab of their choice before my American friends corrupted me.

A few weeks before my birthday, my parents set up a meeting with a man from the Middle East. He was a Lebanese Arab, a Sunni Muslim. My parents were not too thrilled with the idea of marrying me off to a Sunni, since the Sunni version of Islam is quite different from the Shia tradition, but he was an Arab, and that would suffice as long as he could pay the bride price. They were asking for fifty thousand dollars. He was introduced to me as Samir Ali. He was blonde and blue-eyed and very attractive, but he was not attractive enough for me to marry. I refused.

That was the wrong thing to do. I had already rejected my cousin and other men. My father could not believe it.

"How stupid can you be?" he yelled angrily. "How many times do I have to beat you? How many times do I have to tell you? You're not going to marry an American. I'll kill you if you don't marry an Arab. What's wrong with Samir? Why won't you marry him?"

"For a lot of reasons, Baba. You don't understand. I don't know him. I don't love him. I don't want to get married at all. I'm still only fifteen. I want to graduate and go to college, get my own apartment, and be a movie star. Beat me if you want to, but I won't change my mind. You can't make me do it!" I was crying and screaming at my father.

He left me for a minute and came back with his favorite belt and proceeded to flog me in the usual manner. He used the belt like he was whipping a horse, lashing my body from top to bottom. "You want to be a movie star? You're going to be nothing!" He was yelling in my face. I had welts all over, and I looked horrid. The belt marks were like tire tracks. Every move I made was painful. I was exhausted from the beating and had to miss school for several days. The report to school was that I was not feeling well.

Many suitors came, and I rejected all of them—every last one—and suffered the consequences. It did not matter to me that the bride price would have made my parents financially comfortable. Almost every week there was a different man trying to make me his wife. One story in particular bears telling.

Shortly after I rejected Samir, a Palestinian Arab named Fahad was found for me. My parents set the bride price at sixty-five thousand dollars. Fahad wanted desperately to become an American citizen so he did not mind paying that kind of money.

When Fahad arrived, I immediately noticed that he was different from the other suitors. All the others (except for Assam in Lebanon) were at least somewhat close to my age, but Fahad was about twenty years older than I was! We were introduced, and he asked my father if he could take me to the Fox Theatre in downtown Detroit to see a movie.

I was already familiar with the Fox. Once, when my parents thought I had gone to visit my friend, Karen, I took a bus to Detroit to see a French movie with my friends, Teresa and Donna. About halfway through the movie, there was a scene of two gorgeous, young women taking a shower together and kissing. My friends and I were shocked! We had not seen anything like that before! One of the lesbians was named Nadia. That is how I discovered that my name was of French origin. Anyway, this would be the second time for me at the Fox Theatre. I really did not want to go, but I agreed in order to pacify my parents.

The movie started around eight thirty, so Fahad picked me up around eight o'clock. I have no recollection of what was showing. I remember being extremely bored. I wanted to leave. Furthermore, I did not like the way things were going with Fahad. He made several attempts to put his arm around me, and each time I lifted it off. About a half hour into the movie, I asked Fahad to excuse me. I said I needed to use the restroom, and I would be right back.

Instead of going to the restroom, I left the theater and hailed a cab. "How much will it cost to take me to Dearborn?" I asked. "

"About ten dollars," the driver said, "but you shouldn't be out late at night like this. Is anyone with you?"

"No, I'm here alone," I replied, "but I don't have enough money to go back home."

The driver was a good man and was worried about me. "Hop in," he said. "It's all right. I'll take you home. It's dangerous for you to be out on the streets alone. I'd never forgive myself if I heard that something happened to you."

"Thank you, thank you, sir," I replied. "I really appreciate your concern." He took me right to my door.

It was already about nine thirty. I wondered how Fahad was enjoying the movie by himself. I sneaked upstairs and went straight to bed. I had been asleep for a while when the commotion downstairs woke me. My parents were shouting and cursing. When they took a breath, I recognized Fahad's voice. It was agitated but he was not shouting. I heard him say that he had lost me. More shouting and cursing by my parents ensued. Fahad was doing his best to explain that he had looked everywhere after I did not return from the restroom, but he could not find me. He also said that he called the police and reported me missing. I decided to go downstairs to settle the matter.

I could say that they were surprised to see me, but it would be more accurate to say that I could have blown them over like blowing out candles on a birthday cake. They were jaw-dropping stunned. You might think after all the hullabaloo that I would have been engulfed with hugs and kisses now that the lost was found, but no. Instead, my father yelled at me, "What are you doing home?"

"I was sleeping."

"How did you get here?"

"I took a cab. A nice cab driver took me all the way home and didn't charge me a nickel." I told them the whole story factually, except for one small detail at the end. I crafted a lie to save my neck. I told them that Fahad was trying to kiss me, and I was afraid that he might try to do something more.

"That's why I left him in the theatre and came home," I explained. These few words elicited another round of cursing and shouting, and the ruse worked for a short while, but it soon turned against me. My fate was sealed when Fahad swore on his mother's grave that he was innocent. Swearing on someone's grave, especially your mother's, pretty much ends a discussion among Arabs. Fahad played his ace, and my parents believed him. My father immediately took off his belt and began hitting me with it.

I screamed at Fahad, "This is all your fault. I don't want to marry you!"

Fahad mercifully intervened on my behalf, despite the way I had set him up. "Your daughter doesn't want me, and I won't let her be forced," he insisted. He was a man of conscience and compassion. Fahad begged my father to leave me alone. He did, at least for that night, and things remained calm until the next Friday.

My friend Teresa's birthday was also in May, a week before mine. Her parents were giving her a sweet-sixteen party. "I'll be lucky if my father doesn't kill me before I'm sixteen," I told Teresa. Certainly there would be no party. Still, I wanted to attend Teresa's party, so I asked my parents if I could go. The response was predictable.

"Who's going?" they asked.

"Just kids from school."

"How about boys? Will they be there?"

"I suppose so, probably Teresa's boyfriend, his friends, maybe some others."

"Absolutely not! If there are boys, you can't go!" They were adamant.

I let the words fly right past me. I planned to go anyway. I did not care about the consequences. It was my best friend's birthday party, and I was determined to be there.

The party was scheduled to begin at six o'clock the next evening. It was going to be an all-night party, so Teresa told me to come whenever I could. She knew what would happen if I were caught at her party. She was worried about it, but I convinced her that I would not miss it.

I sneaked over to Teresa's around eight o'clock, hoping my parents would think that I was upstairs in my bedroom doing homework. Most of my friends from school were already at the party when I arrived. Billy was there, too. It was good to see him, since I had not seen him for a while. I missed him. We talked and played some games together, and everyone played spin the bottle. I was having so much fun that I forgot to watch the clock.

During the spin the bottle game, my mother was outside Teresa's house knocking at the side door. She had looked through the basement window and saw how spin the bottle was played, with the kissing and all. And, of course, she saw that the boys were American. It would not have made any difference if they had been Martians. She was livid. She continued to knock on the side door. Not getting a response, she let herself in. She called out my name and told me to come outside. Before I could reach the door, she grabbed me by the hair, yelled obscenities at me, and dragged me home two blocks, pulling my hair, beating and punching me the whole way.

"Didn't we tell you that you couldn't go the party? You liar," she screamed.

"She's my best friend," I complained. "It's her sixteenth birthday party, and I didn't do anything bad."

My father called me a whore and beat me with the belt again. Then he went to the kitchen table, picked up the pepper-shaker, unscrewed the lid, and poured the entire contents into my mouth. I tried to fight him off but could not do it. The pepper went into my eyes, and my throat was packed with it like a stuffed turkey. I could not talk. I struggled for breath. I rushed into the bathroom and tried to cough up the pepper. I rinsed my mouth with cold water, hoping to find relief that way, but it did not help much, so I drank water to dissolve the plug of pepper packed in my throat. I drank and drank and drank. My mother even tried to help, seeing the danger I was in. My eyes were burning, and I could not see for hours. Oh, God, I was miserable! By some miracle, I did not inhale the pepper, for I very well might have died of asphyxiation. The burning in my mouth and throat lasted for days.

My mother felt bad about this extreme punishment, but she would not stand up for me, and she was not willing to give me the freedom to be a teenager, to have friends, to make some choices for myself. My father never had remorse for any of the punishments he dished out. Nothing was too severe for him. He never showed regret or sadness. He did everything in his power to break my will. He was going to show me that it was his way or no way.

I learned to deal with it. As I said before, the mind is a wonderful thing. I never left my Dream Girl role that I assumed when I was eight years old; I just revived it when necessary. I learned to survive by filling my mind with things I liked. It is how I kept my sanity. I always turned to music and dance and dreamed about being a movie star. I listened to all kinds of music and watched Dick Clark's *American Bandstand* every day after school. I looked forward to seeing all the kids dancing and having fun. I envisioned myself on the show, dancing and meeting Ricky Nelson, Otis Redding, Lionel Ritchie, and all the others. That was my dream.

School was a great escape, too. I was with all of my friends there. Only a few of them knew how bad things were at home for me. As for the others, even if they had heard about the severity of my life, they would not have understood; they were all Americans. I never heard that any of them got beatings for making friends. They were free to live. I tried to keep my life at home a secret. My parents warned me that if I told anyone they would send me to Lebanon, and I could never come back to America.

On one occasion, I made the mistake of telling one of my teachers that I had been locked up in my bedroom for a whole day without any food to eat. Did I pay for that! The teacher called my parents. I was an embarrassment to the family. I shamed them. Why did I tell the teacher what was done to me? More beatings followed, and I missed school for another two days.

Unless I was beaten up so badly that I could not walk, I always went to school, no matter what. I looked forward to school, to homework assignments, and to escaping to the library whenever I could to read and study. Never mind the fear of being caught. I loved to read. Reading was a great escape. One of my favorite books was *Little Women*, by Louisa May Alcott. What a great story! There was so much love in that family, and the daughters were treasured. I never knew anything like that existed. It was certainly beyond my experience. I thought the book was just a fantasy. Real people did not love their children like that.

Because I had to repeat kindergarten (due to not knowing English well), and because of the year in Lebanon, I graduated ninth grade at age sixteen. I'll never forget that day, because I was asked to be the mistress of ceremonies for the commencement program. I was so nervous. When I got to the podium, all I could do was giggle. My favorite teacher did not help the situation. He was behind the curtain, prompting me and laughing the whole time. The more he prompted and laughed, the more I giggled. The audience loved it. They laughed and laughed until they were all out of control. I finally gave my commencement speech, and I got a standing ovation!

The Beatles craze was on, and I listened to all their songs. At first I did not care much for *I Want To Hold Your Hand,* because the same lyrics were repeated over and over again, but it grew on me, and I came to like it as much as their other hits. My favorites were all topping the charts: *Can't Buy Me Love, Twist and Shout, She Loves You,* and *Please, Please Me.*

The Beatles arrived at the newly named John F. Kennedy Airport in February 1964. Three thousand screaming fans greeted them. Two days later I saw them on the *Ed Sullivan Show.* Some newspapers reported that the Beatles craze would not last, but I knew it would. Thousands of people do not scream for nothing.

I enjoyed going to the movies also whenever I could. A ticket cost only twenty-five cents. Whenever I went, I always reminded myself that someday I would be up there on the big screen, too. Someday.

I continued to collect records and a lot of movie magazines. I bought *Radio-TV Mirror Magazine, Photoplay,* and several others. They were great because they all had 8x10 glamour photos of the movie stars and bios about them. Most of the stars had fan clubs, and I wrote to every one. I looked forward to receiving an autographed black and white photograph either for free or for a dollar. I had a lot of pictures of my favorite movie stars and singers: Marilyn Monroe, Ava Gardner, Susan Hayward, Lana Turner, Elvis, Bobby Rydell, Fabian, and a lot more. I pasted their pictures and articles about them in scrapbooks that I made with colored construction paper. I looked at them almost every night, especially when I was in pain from beatings. They took my mind off my situation and helped me to dream of freedom, of being a star in Hollywood, of a better life.

At first we find it hard to face,
Like aliens from another place,
The changing elements, the snow,
The cold precipitation.

Aliens

SCHOOL WAS OUT AND I HAD JUST PASSED MY sixteenth birthday. The coming year would bring a lot of changes. My father insisted that I get a job, so, after only a day or two, I got hired at Blazo's Drive-In as a carhop. Blazo's was a cool place to be, as everyone from school came there for a hamburger and a shake. It was a lot of fun to see boys with their girlfriends at Blazo's, eating and laughing and having a good time. I envied them and wanted to date and go for a hamburger just like them.

One day something strange happened. A shiny, new sports car came into Blazo's. It was a red Corvette. I went up to the car to take an order. The driver was a very handsome young man with blonde hair and blue eyes.

"Hey, gorgeous, what's your name?" he asked.

"Nadia," I replied with a big, happy smile. "What's yours?"

"I'm Johnnie, Johnnie Temple. Everyone calls me J.T. I'm a manager for a magazine company. We recruit girls and guys to

Breakaway

sell our magazines door to door all over the country. How much do you make here?"

"Just minimum wage and tips. Why?"

"How would you like to make over five hundred dollars a month?"

"That would be great."

"You're too pretty to work here and earn so little." Then he lowered his voice to almost a whisper and asked, "How old are you?"

"Sixteen," I said proudly. "I just turned sixteen."

"Sixteen, that's okay. You're a minor, but if your parents sign papers giving me guardianship, I can hire you. Do you think they'll let you go?"

"I hope so, but I doubt it."

I gave J.T. my address and phone number. I was really naïve then. J.T. came over and spoke to my parents. They visited a long time, and my parents liked him. He gained their trust right away. He said he was from Minnesota. He was a very smooth talker. My father's eyes lit up when J.T. told him how much money I would be making. Fifteen hundred dollars in three months! I was shocked that my father would let me go, but he saw me as a source of cash. So my parents agreed to make J.T. my guardian, and I was good to go. It was a miracle. I would be free of beatings and suitors for a whole summer. This was my chance to meet new people and see new places, especially California. I was so excited; I could not sleep the whole night. I was going to work and be far away from home. All I had to do was give my parents the money. I was happy enough to buy my freedom.

I did not have much packing to do as most of what I wore was shared with my sisters. I never got a new pair of shoes unless the old ones had a hole in the sole. My mother would let me pick my shoes as long as they did not cost more than a dollar. If there was a clearance sale, I might get lucky and buy two pairs. It was fun buying shoes. Some were pointed and some square-toed. I especially liked the pointed shoes; they looked so feminine and dainty. So I began packing for my trip. I looked at it as sort of a vacation. Although my father fully expected me to send home whatever money I earned, I planned to keep some of it. He would never know the difference.

When the departure day arrived, J.T. picked me up in a rented sedan, and we drove to a staging area. About fifty teenagers were there. We were divided up into ten teams. Each team had its own manager who was also the driver. I went with J.T. and four other kids.

We went first to Columbus, Ohio, where we spent the night. The next morning, five teams gathered at a restaurant for breakfast. We were told the other teams were elsewhere in the city. We had specific territories and quotas to meet. Each team would compete with the other teams. We were given a script to say to people to get them to buy magazines from us. The script went something like this:

"Hi, my name is Nadia, how are you today? I'm in a contest with a lot of other kids to earn money for my college education. The more magazines you buy, the more points I get. The person with the most points wins a full scholarship. I could be the winner with your help. I really want to win, so will you help me?"

Almost all of the people I met were gracious and kind. They welcomed me into their homes. They liked me, trusted me, and wanted to help me win the contest. When I finished with the script, I would sit and talk with them for a few minutes. Most of them were willing to buy the magazine subscriptions and give me a deposit toward their order. The balance would be billed to them. I was surprised that people trusted me so much and gave me their money.

I met a lot of nice people. I imagined that someday I would visit them all again. I kept a notebook with their names, addresses, and phone numbers, so I could keep in touch with them. I wanted to be sure that they were happy with the magazines that would start arriving in about a month.

The hours seemed to fly by until it was quitting time when I went to the designated site to join my manager and teammates. We headed in the direction of Chicago, our next major stop where we would pick up Route 66, the so-called Main Street of America, and stay on it most of the way to California. However, we had several cities to cover in Ohio and Indiana before reaching Chicago. On the way to our next stop, J.T. asked all of us on my team, one by one, how we did. When it was my turn, he asked, "How about you, Nadia, how did you do today?"

"Well, I collected over a thousand dollars in deposits. Is that good?"

"Is that good?" J.T. was ecstatic. "It's fabulous! You're fabulous! I'm sure you collected more than anyone else on all the teams." He was thrilled beyond anything I expected. "You're a natural. I knew it. I knew it," he gushed. "I knew that when people met you they would trust you. I'm so proud of you." His enthusiasm lifted my spirit, and I felt great. Nobody was ever that proud of me.

We had meetings every day. We were told in detail not only what to say, but how to speak, how to pause, how to ask key questions, how to measure interest by the customer's nonverbal communication, when to stop the interview, how to close the deal, where to meet at the end of the day, and, most importantly, to bring all the deposit money to our team leader. Those who reached their quotas were promised special bonuses.

We were on the road for a month when it came time for payday. I was so excited I could hardly stand it. It would have taken all summer to earn five hundred dollars at Blazo's. I had reached my quotas every day and more. I planned to send the five hundred to my parents, but I was going to keep the bonuses. I had already decided how I was going to spend the money. None of us kids had received a check yet, so I asked J.T. about it.

"It takes a lot of money to run this operation," he said. "Where do you think the money goes? Whatever you collect every day goes into the pot and pays for our travel. It goes to hotels, food, gas, and other expenses. You won't get a check until people get their magazines and pay the balances they owe for their subscriptions. You should all be getting paychecks next month."

That satisfied us. We were so naïve. We would just wait for another month for our money. We were all green, all except one.

She was a couple of years my senior, and she became a close friend, sort of a surrogate mother to me. She was a tall, slender girl with chestnut brown hair and hazel green eyes. Her face was lightly freckled and dainty. She was very pretty, and she was savvy. She knew her way around, especially with the opposite sex, and she took it as her sacred duty to protect me. Her name was Rachel Williams. She was born in a small town in Kentucky. Her parents owned the local newspaper.

As time went on, I learned that our close friendship had a common factor named J.T. He was my manager and her crush. While she was crushing him, she also knew that he had a crush on me. Eventually, she told me that he was waiting until I turned eighteen, and then he would make his move. Rachel always knew what he was doing. They were close and he shared his feelings for me with her. She had to protect me from him, she always said, and since she was interested in him herself, the assignment was not all that bad. J.T., it turned out, was married the entire time. He was really from Missouri and was separated from his wife. He rationalized his philandering by saying that he was on the road most of the time, and it was not good for the marriage.

Anyway, wherever I went, whatever I did, there was Rachel like a shadow, following me and watching every move I made. She was always watching J.T., too, worried that he might try to seduce me. She was my self-designated guardian angel. I really was naïve about sex. I had that short, unfinished tutorial with Billy on the steps of the hotel, but I did not have any firsthand knowledge about boys and what their real intentions were. I knew that it took more than kissing to get pregnant, but I didn't know exactly what or how. You could say I was sexually illiterate. Virgin I was in mind and body. So Rachel took me under her wing. As long as she was there, I felt secure. I was happy for her friendship.

We were selling our way to California when we stopped at a little roadside café for lunch somewhere in western Missouri, not too far from the Kansas state line. After lunch, we were told to saddle up, so to speak, because we needed to get to Leavenworth, Kansas, before dark. We all got into our respective vehicles and off we went, doing what we always did on every trip: we sang, we talked, and we laughed.

It was a lot of fun listening to the radio and singing along with our favorite artists. Rachel and I sat in the front seat. Most cars had bench seats in the front in those days. I sat by the window, and she sat next to J.T. for my protection. Scottie, Tim, and Ann shared the back seat. We had a good time singing: *Town Without Pity*, *The Wanderer*, *Volare*, *Johnny B. Goode*, and other great hits. We could not wait to get to California. Hollywood was on my mind. My dream was coming true. I hoped to see Dion, Annette Funicello, or Bobby Rydell. I let my imagination run wild as we passed through the rolling hills of western Missouri and the outskirts of Kansas City.

We arrived in Leavenworth, Kansas, home of the famous United States Penitentiary, around five o'clock in the afternoon. The city looked old, kind of like a cowboy town—like in the westerns my father watched on TV—but it was charming. J.T. said it was a good time to visit the folks there; they would be at home getting ready to have dinner. So one by one he dropped us off at each street corner in a quiet residential area. I was told to meet J.T. two blocks away in two hours. It was a typical mid-western neighborhood with tree-lined streets. But nobody was on the streets. This was unusual to me and kind of scary. I was a city girl. I was used to seeing people everywhere. I knocked at a door, and an elderly woman answered. She was about seventy-five years old. She wore her gray hair tied in a bun, and her granny glasses were balanced precariously on her nose. Her skin was wrinkled and tired. I could tell that she had worked hard all of her life.

"Can I help ya?" she said as she opened the door.

"Yes," I mumbled nervously. I did not want to sell magazines to this woman. She looked so poor. I just could not do it. "My name is Nadia. I came by to see if you're all right."

"What did you say? I can't hear too good, speak louder," she shouted and pointed to her ear.

"*Okay, my name is Nadia. I just came by to see if you're okay.*" I was almost yelling.

"*What did you say, dear?*" She must have been stone deaf.

"*Thanks, anyway, I have to go. I'll see you later.*"

I ran off her porch and waved a friendly goodbye as I left her yard and moved on to the next house. When I knocked on the door, a young man in his early twenties opened it. His father was standing behind him. They asked me to "Come on in and how can we help ya?"

I gave my canned introduction as usual. They were very friendly and agreed to buy some magazines. As I was leaving, I asked for their phone number so I could keep in touch. I liked them. They were good to me. Time passed quickly as I continued knocking on doors and selling. By the time I was finished with my street, it was beginning to get dark, so I headed back to meet J.T.

When I got to our meeting spot, there was no J.T. I looked up and down the street and decided to walk a bit to look for him. Before long, I began to panic. I began to walk faster as it got darker, looking behind me often to see if anyone was following me. Then I started to run. I was scared, but I had to be bold and brave. Darkness had fallen, and no one was in sight. Where was J.T.? Where were the rest of my teammates? I ran until I was out of breath, my pulse pounding in my ears.

I made my way out of the residential neighborhood until I came to a little strip center. There was a store that sold cowboy boots and clothes, a Laundromat, and two antique stores. I tried the doors of these establishments, but they were all closed. The whole town seemed to be asleep. All the lights were turned off. It was very eerie.

Suddenly, the silence was broken. Two police cars were coming down the street with their sirens screaming and lights flashing. I instinctively hid inside the doorway of a store. The cars stopped right in front of my store, and four officers jumped out and came toward me. One of the officers shouted: "Leavenworth

Police. We saw you go in there. Come out now, young lady. Don't resist or you'll go to jail."

"Are they talking to me," I asked myself. I could not believe it. I was paralyzed with fear, except my knees were weak and shaking. When I finally mustered the courage to move and step out of the doorway, the officers came toward me.

"Are you looking for me?" I asked, my voice trembling. One of the officers flashed a light in my face.

"Yes, you're the one. We have your manager and the rest of your friends at the station. They told us you were out here alone. Let's go." They put me in the back seat of one of the squad cars, and off we went. It was my first ride in a squad car, but it would not be my last. I was petrified.

We spent what seemed to be an eternity waiting at the police station. We kids just sat like stumps, scared that we might be going to jail, while the officers took the managers aside and talked to them. Finally, when the officers had finished lecturing J.T. and the others, we were released and told to get out of town immediately. They told us that if we were seen in Leavenworth again, they would put us all in jail—no questions asked.

Coincidentally, on the way to Leavenworth we had sung about the town. It was a town without pity. We were happy to leave.

We learn that change is part of life.
Although it comes through pain or strife,
We trust our roots to hold us fast
Through storm or conflagration.

California Dreaming

A MONTH PASSED AS WE TRAVELED FROM CITY to city and state to state selling magazines. Rachel was now closer to J.T. and seemed to have enlisted him to his true role as my guardian. He still had feelings for me, and I liked him, but only as a friend. I met a lot of nice boys and enjoyed the late night parties with bands and dancing that were organized periodically by the managers, but J.T. and Rachel were always on their guard. There was no chance of my being independent, not until we reached California.

We stayed on Route 66 most of the way through Oklahoma, Texas, New Mexico, and Arizona. I was so excited when we crossed the California state line. I was looking for movie stars and rock and roll singers in every car and on every sidewalk, even in the little towns like Needles, Amboy, Barstow, and Victorville. Today Amboy is a ghost town in the Mojave Desert, but it was a major stop on Route 66 before Interstate 40 was built in the 1970s. We stopped at Roy's Motel and Café for gas, but no movie stars were there. I still thought it was worth looking for them!

After some selling in San Bernardino and Riverside, we arrived in Anaheim where we checked into a large motel on Katella Avenue near Disneyland. It was not fancy but it was clean, and it must have been cheap as J.T. said we would be staying there for at least two weeks. Then we would move on to another city.

At the end of our first week there, the managers got together and planned a party for Saturday night. They said it was in honor of our outstanding sales efforts. They hired a local band with a lead singer who was supposed to be really good. The managers made it sound like a lot of fun. After Friday night dinner with the gang, I went to my room. Rachel was my roommate, but she sometimes just said good night and then left to spend the night with J.T. Tonight was one of those nights, so I turned out the light and went to sleep thinking about the party.

I got up early and was ready to go for breakfast, but Rachel had not returned, so I knocked on J.T.'s door to wake them up.

"Hey, I'm hungry. Let's go to breakfast," I yelled at the door. I knocked loudly, but no one responded. I could hear Rachel moaning inside.

"We'll be there. Give us ten minutes," she finally replied tersely.

"Do you need help?" I was concerned about the moaning.

"*No!*" The voice was hurried.

"Shall I call a doctor?" I persisted.

"*No! No!!*" The voice was more agitated.

"Are you sure? Nothing I can do? Shall I get the manager?" I was really getting worried.

"*No! No! No! Just give us a few minutes!*" The voice was exasperated and breathless.

"Okay, I'll wait in the room." They clearly did not want my help.

Breakfast was uneventful, although Rachel and J.T. had a kind of peculiar look about them. The rest of the day was spent having meetings with the managers. The talk was mostly about quotas and whether we had made them or not. However, nothing was said about paychecks, so I asked Rachel about it again. She said to be patient, and eventually we would all get paid. It seemed useless to talk about money, so I decided to turn my thoughts to the party. It was going to start at eight o'clock.

I went to the party room an hour early to get a good seat. There would be fifty kids in addition to the managers, and I did not want to be stuck at the back of the room. The band was getting set up when I got there. The drum set was already in place. Big letters on the bass drum spelled *The Casey Wild Band*.

The band had three members. Casey was the lead guitarist and singer, Jack was the drummer, and Rick was on keyboards. All three guys were really cool. Casey was especially cute. Both he and Rick were twenty years old, and Jack was twenty-three. They played mostly Chuck Berry hits like *Johnny B. Goode*, *Around and Around*, *Maybellene,* and *Sweet Little Sixteen*, as well as a few other songs like Johnny Cash's *I Walk The Line*.

Casey and I clicked immediately. He was the handsomest guy I had seen during the whole trip. Plus, he was older and mature and smart. Casey sat with me during his breaks, and we talked about my job. J.T. and Rachel were hovering and noticed Casey getting a little too close to me, so Rachel called me over and told me to be careful.

"Rachel, he's so nice to me. He listens to me and asks a lot of questions about what I want to do, where I'll be going next, and what makes me happy. He's harmless. Don't worry."

"Okay," Rachel replied. "Just be careful. He's older than you and has been around."

"Okay, Rachel, and thanks."

I rejoined Ann, Tim, and Scottie at our table. I enjoyed their company, since I had spent so much time with them on the road. Casey played one more set, and I danced with the boys. When the set was over, Casey joined me. We sat by the pool and talked for a long time. Casey told me how much he liked me. He also said I should not be involved with a magazine crew.

"You could do so much more with your life right now," he said. "You told me they haven't paid you yet. You also said that you called a few of the people who bought the magazines from you, and no one has received them. Something's wrong here. Where's all that money?"

"I don't know, Casey, but I feel bad about all those people who trusted me."

"It's not your fault," remarked Casey. "You didn't know. You did what you were told to do, but you don't need to do it anymore. How would you like to leave with Jack and me? You can stay with Jack's sister, Tonya, and her husband in Whittier. You'll like them, and I know they'll love to have you there. You can help me compose my lyrics, and I promise not to do anything you don't want to do. Think about it. I'm leaving in the morning. Let me know if you decide to go with us."

"Okay, I will. I'll think it over tonight. I'll see you in the morning and give you my decision." I wondered if this might be my opportunity to stay in California, to go to Hollywood and do what I had dreamed of since I was ten years old. I fell asleep with my clothes on, thinking and dreaming of what could happen tomorrow.

"Nadia, Nadia, wake up. What time did you come into the room last night?" asked Rachel quietly.

"I don't know, somewhere around one o'clock, I guess. I know it was late. I must have fallen asleep while I was thinking about things," I replied.

"What's on your mind, sweetheart?" Rachel had such a kind manner.

"Well, Rachel, Casey likes me, and I like him. I'm thinking about leaving with him and quitting this business. I haven't been paid, and I really would like to stay here. I love California. This is my dream, my chance to be free."

"But you're only sixteen and naïve in many ways. Casey is a lot older than you. Did you tell him that you're a virgin?"

"No, of course not. How can I tell him something like that? He thinks I'm pretty and smart, and he knows about everything that goes on here."

"Did you tell him about J.T. and me?" Rachel seemed nervous.

"No, but he knows about the money that seems to have disappeared, about orders that haven't been delivered, about the people who have been cheated, about no paychecks, and, well, I guess he knows about everything except you and J.T." She looked like the air had been let out of her.

"Okay, okay," she replied. "You do what you want, but it might not be easy to leave. You know how J.T. feels about you."

"I won't tell him. I'll just leave. Let me go and tell Casey, and I'll be back for my clothes." I loved Rachel, so leaving her was bittersweet. We hugged and kissed each other with tears in our eyes.

I knocked on Casey's door, but there was no answer. Was I too late? Had he left already, thinking I was not going with him? "Please, Casey, please be here. Where are you? Where are you, Casey?" I spoke my thoughts aloud. I looked for him in the lobby and by the pool but without success. Finally, I checked the back parking lot. He was there loading his equipment and securing the trailer in back of his truck. He saw me coming and waved.

"Hi, Nadia, I'll be right there. Just give me a few minutes, okay?" I was used to this line by now, so I went back to wait in the lobby. Casey and Jack came in shortly with big grins on their faces, as if they knew that my decision was to leave with them.

"Well, are you coming with us or not?" Casey asked.

"I'm going with you, but I'm scared. Are you sure your sister won't mind, Jack?"

"Not at all," he replied. "I called her and she's looking forward to meeting you."

"In that case, it's done. I'm going with you."

"Great," enthused Casey. "Let's go get your suitcase and scram out of here."

"Okay, Casey, take my suitcase first, and put it in your truck. I'll come to the back lot and join you in a couple of minutes. Then that's it. We're gone. I didn't tell my manager that I'm leaving with you. It's a little difficult, because he likes me a lot."

"Good idea," Casey said, "let's go. We don't want any problems."

Just as I was handing Casey my suitcase, J.T. appeared out of nowhere.

"What are you doing here? Where do you think you're going?" He was hopping mad.

"She's coming with me," Casey said. *"She's coming with me right now."*

"No, she isn't. She's staying right here." J.T. was turning tomato red.

" J.T.," I said as firmly as I could, "I'm leaving with Casey and Jack. I've decided to quit this job."

"You're not leaving with them, and that's it," yelled J.T.

Some other managers heard the ruckus and came to help J.T. They burst into my room, dragged Casey outside, and pushed me back inside. Then they slammed the door shut and locked the deadbolt from the outside, so I could not get out.

"Let me out of here!" I screamed. *"Let me out of here!"* Hot tears were streaming down my face. I tried the window and found that I could open it, so I climbed out. There was a crowd of kids by the pool. Casey and J.T. were in a fistfight over me. Oh, my God! What had I done? Someone was going to get hurt, and it was my fault.

The front desk manager called the police. Casey and J.T. were still fighting when they arrived. Both guys were cut and bleeding. Casey had a gash above his right eye, and J.T.'s lip looked like a blown-out tire. We explained the situation to the police as delicately as possible so the magazine crew would not be investigated for fraud. Finally, the police left it up to me. They asked me if I wanted to stay or leave. I looked at Rachel and J.T. and said, "I love you both, but I have to leave."

Breakaway

So I left with J.T. and Rachel both in tears. J.T. handed me his card and told me to call him if I changed my mind. Casey took me by the hand, opened the truck door for me, and circled to the driver's side. Jack was already waiting in the truck. Off we went to Whittier. What a day!

Whittier, California, is a town well known for its celebrities and for the fact that the world's largest cemetery is located there. Richard Nixon played football at Whittier High School and Whittier College. The town looked fabulous to me. I loved the houses, one subdivision after another. Palm trees lined the streets, and there were a lot of parks. It was so tropical. I had read about Whittier in my movie magazines.

"Are there any movie stars here?" I asked.

"Sure, lots of them," Jack answered. "A lot of TV shows and movies have been filmed here." Jack was a quiet guy. He had black hair, coal-black eyes, and skin as white as snow. He was very humble, honest, and sincere.

Casey was so handsome that he could have been a teenage idol or a rock and roll singer. He had black hair and brown eyes, long lashes, and a perfect nose. His hair was combed like Elvis Presley's and he was about as tall, somewhere around six feet or so. He was polished, a real gentleman. He treated me like a lady. He opened and closed doors for me, helped me in and out the truck, and was always kind and gentle. I reflected on my new situation as we arrived at our destination. It was great to have two nice guys treating me like a princess.

Casey pulled the truck to a stop in the driveway of a lovely home. Jack got his key out and opened the door to his sister's house. "Come on in and make yourself comfortable," he said. Tonya and her husband were still at work. I had never seen a more beautiful house. It was a huge, one-story ranch that went on and on. The decorating was gorgeous: beautiful wood and tile floors, elegant furniture, two fireplaces, gleaming kitchen appliances, and all the rooms were enormous.

"This looks like a palace," I said. Casey and Jack laughed at my innocence. I still had not seen much of life.

"No, it's just a big house. A lot of the houses here are big like this."

"How many bedrooms are there?"

"Four."

"How many bathrooms?"

"Four." Jack could not refrain from smiling.

I told them that at home I had to share my bedroom and my bed with two sisters. Our house had four bedrooms and three bathrooms, but it was not so big and beautiful and luxurious. We only had one bathroom upstairs for all of us kids to use. My parents had their own bathroom and bedroom downstairs, and there was a bathroom in the basement. I rambled on. They just listened and laughed. I knew then, without a doubt, that I had made the right decision to leave the magazine crew. I was going to be somebody, and this was the beginning of a new life for me.

Casey lived in a studio apartment on Whittier Boulevard. Every day for a month he came over to Tonya's house to rehearse his songs with Jack. They would start in the afternoon and work late into the night. I spent about four hours each day listening to them and working on the lyrics. They were amazed at the speed of my handwriting. I have always been a fast writer and an excellent speller. The best years of my childhood at school were grades three through six. I loved winning spelling bees and memorizing poetry. I had jumbo gold stars all across the board for reading, spelling, and reciting poetry. I loved the opportunity to read aloud to the class. My hand was always first to go up. My teachers had high hopes for me.

At the end of the month, I had two notebooks of handwritten lyrics ready for the band. They rehearsed while Tonya and her husband, Will, and I sat and listened. Everything seemed to be going well until a friend of theirs came over. He had red curly hair, green eyes, and freckles. He was really cute. He was about six feet tall. All the guys in California seemed to be over six feet. His name was Jerry Stone. Jerry was introduced to me, and we got along great right from the start.

"How would you like to go bowling with me sometime?" he asked kind of shyly.

"I'd love to go bowling. I've never done that."

"What! You've never been bowling?"

"That's right. I've never even been on a date."

"Okay, Nadia, tomorrow I'll pick you up at six o'clock. We'll go to dinner first and then bowling."

"That's great," I said happily. "I'll be ready, thanks."

Jerry left after spending an hour or so with us. What a nice guy! I asked Tonya a lot of questions about him. She said that he was nineteen, was very smart, and was attending college. He planned to be a lawyer someday.

I had never met so many nice people. This was all new to me. I had freedom to date, and I had freedom to be myself.

The next day, Jerry picked me up and we went bowling, but I did not tell Casey about my date. I was afraid to. I did not want him to get mad at me, so I said nothing. I did not think he would come over while I was gone, but Casey and Jack were waiting to talk to me when I came home.

"Nadia, what are you doing going out with guys you don't even know?" Jack asked with a worried look.

"Tonya knows Jerry, and she said it would be all right. We just had dinner and went bowling." Casey did not say anything. He just looked sad. I knew I had hurt his feelings. "Don't worry, I won't go out with Jerry again." What I could not tell them was that Jerry planned to take me out again in two days. I did not know how to call him and say I could not go. I thought I would wait until he came over, and then I would say no.

Well, when the time came, I could not do it. Jerry rang the doorbell, but I did not answer it. I just let him ring and ring. Finally, he left, and I felt lousy. I wished that I had opened the door and been honest with him. Why didn't I do that? Jerry called me later that evening and asked me why I didn't answer the door. He knew I was there. I explained the situation with Casey, and he said he did not like it, but he understood. He said he was not aware that Casey and I were together, but, if things did not work out, I should call him. I apologized and told him I liked him a lot.

Summer was going fast, and it was already the last week of July. I had to go back to school, but I didn't want to think of that now. I was too busy trying to help Casey and Jack. One day, I decided to have Jack take me to Casey's place to surprise him. I had never gone there. I did not think it would look good for a sixteen-year-old to be seen going into an apartment building by herself. Jack drove me there, and we entered the lobby together. I was really nervous as we knocked on Casey's door.

"Who's there?" Casey yelled from the apartment.

"It's me, open up," Jack shouted. Then he leaned over to me and whispered, "Shhhhh, don't say anything." Casey opened the door and was shocked to see me standing there. He slammed the door right away and then opened it back up a crack.

"What's going on, Casey?" Jack asked.

"You didn't tell me Nadia was with you," Casey replied nervously.

"Well, hello, little girl!" A soft, sweet voice resonated from a blonde who appeared at the door. "Who are you? I'm Doris, so what's your name, darlin'?"

"Nadia," I said, and my mouth felt as dry as dust. I was naïve enough, but I knew by now that a woman did not stay with a man in his room without having slept with him. I tried to stay calm, but my Arab temper was running hot. Doris had her hair up in a twist and was wearing gold pants and a gold blouse with a leopard print jacket. She looked like a movie star. Under other circumstances, I would have liked to meet her, but at that moment I hated her. I turned away, looked at Jack, and said sarcastically, "Let's go Jack. It looks like Casey is busy right now." I was heartbroken. I really liked Casey. Why had he done this to me? Jack looked at Casey in disbelief. Then he took my hand, and we left to go back home.

Jack was so comforting to me. He tried to explain what was going on with Casey.

"Nadia, he wants you, but you're a minor and a virgin. Casey was just having fun with Doris. He doesn't really care for her; he really wants to be with you, but he did the wrong thing. Nadia, I have to tell you that I like you very much, I mean *very* much. I have from the first time I met you, but you were interested in Casey, not me, so I stepped aside."

"I'm so sorry, Jack," I replied sadly, "I'm really sorry. I like you a lot, too. You're really a great guy, but I'm hurt right now, Jack. I don't even want to see Casey again. He betrayed me. He lied to me. He wanted me to sit at home until I was of age, while he was out playing around with other girls. Jack, I appreciate what you and Tonya have done for me, but tomorrow I'm going to look for a job and move into my own place."

"You're only sixteen so that's going to be hard to do," he said quietly.

"I have to try and see what happens. I can't stay with you forever."

"Okay, Nadia, I'll help you as much as I can."

"Thanks, Jack, I really appreciate it."

In the days that followed, I took long walks down Whittier Boulevard trying to find a job. I called temporary agencies, but they all required me to have a car. I did not understand the importance of having a car in California until I tried to get from one part of the city to another. Without a car in California, I was doomed. I walked and walked looking for a job on the Boulevard. I tried restaurants, hotels, and grocery stores. No one was hiring.

On the other hand, I was getting plenty of offers. Several men tried to pick me up. I went to a restaurant and asked if they were hiring. A patron overheard me and came over with a proposition: "You're a pretty girl, I'd like to help you. I'm a single dad with two children. How would you like to be their nanny?" Green as I was, it was impossible to miss the innuendo that the nanny this man wanted would be doing more than taking care of the children. I looked at him, at his forlorn face, and said, "No thanks, I really appreciate your offer, but I can't do that now."

I left the restaurant and walked past a service station, the same one that I had passed several times before. The attendants always whistled at me and yelled for my attention. I always ignored them until this particular day. A slender young man with sleek, black hair and brown eyes came over to me.

"Hi, has anyone ever told you how pretty you are? What's a girl like you doing around here?" he asked.

"Looking for a job," I said. "I need a job so I can get my own apartment."

"Maybe I can help you," he offered with a smile. "My name's Danny, what's yours?"

"Nadia," I replied.

"Here's my idea, Nadia, take it or leave it. What if I rent an apartment in my name, you live with me, and I'll support you until you find a job?"

"What do I have to do until then?" I asked candidly.

"Just sleep with me and cook my meals, that's all."

"Let me think about it."

"Sure, come by and let me know when you're ready."

"I will," I said, knowing that I would never speak to this guy again. I said goodbye to Danny and thanked him for the offer.

After a week of not finding a job, and with the tension at Tonya's high, I knew I had to get out. Tonya and her husband were having difficulties in their marriage. I needed to find a place of my own. Danny's offer was sounding good to me, except for the part about sleeping with him. He was not ugly, but I had no intention of losing my virginity, to say nothing of the fear of getting pregnant. Besides, Rachel had coached me about some of the nasty sexually transmitted diseases one could catch, and none of them appealed to me.

However, it was clear to me that I needed Danny's apartment, but how could I get the apartment without sleeping with him? I mulled it over until a plan finally came to mind. I met with Danny and informed him that I would take the apartment. He was thrilled! He was so happy that he seemed to levitate. I told him that I needed to find a place right away. He was highly motivated!

Danny rented an apartment a block away from the station. He said he wanted to be close to work so he could visit me during his lunch break. It was the first week in August. Danny paid one month's rent in advance and got the key, only one key. The landlady did not know that two people would be living there. Danny gave me the key and went to work on the night shift. He had traded shifts so he could take care of things with me during the day.

Well, I liked the apartment as soon as I walked in. It was perfect! It was furnished very nicely, the windows were big, and it was clean. There was one bedroom, a small kitchen, and a bath. I stayed in the apartment that night, ruminating on my plan until I finally fell asleep. I reasoned that if I had a place to stay, I would eventually find a job. I never had trouble finding a job in Michigan, so I believed that I could succeed in Whittier. At any rate, some of the pressure was off since the rent was already paid, at least for a month. I fell into a peaceful sleep.

I was awakened in the middle of the night by loud knocking at the door. Danny had decided to spend his "lunch" break with me. It was time to put the plan into effect. I posted myself by the dead-bolted door and let him knock. I could hear him shuffling back and forth on the concrete outside, but I remained silent. "*Nadia, let me in!*" he shouted. I did not answer. He continued to bang on the door until a neighbor yelled at him. Probably out of concern that the neighbor might report him for disturbing the peace, he gave up and left. The plan passed its first test. I still had the apartment and my virginity, but I knew that a bigger test would come in the morning when Danny finished his shift. I went back to sleep.

Loud knocking woke me again around eight o'clock. Danny was being persistent. "Let me in Nadia, or I'll go to the landlady and tell her to give me my money back." I remained quiet. I heard him walk away. I knew that he was hormone driven, but I wondered if the plan might fail. Danny was back at the door in ten minutes, apparently without the landlady.

"Nadia, let me in!" I still did not answer. Danny spoke to the door a couple more times without a response. I heard him walk away again. I peeked through the window and saw him going in the direction of the station. He was shuffling along looking very dejected. I felt sorry for him, but not sorry enough to sacrifice my virginity. The plan passed its second test. Danny's apartment was still mine, and no one was going to share it with me.

I showered, dressed, and went out for breakfast before looking for work, using up the last of my cash for poached eggs, toast, and a cup of coffee. I checked the classifieds, but there was nothing interesting nearby, so I walked the boulevard again. I made all the contacts I could, but no one was hiring. After a fruitless morning, I met another young man, blonde with blue eyes, and very handsome. His name was Paul. He was friendly and kind of shy, but not too shy to introduce himself. He was attracted to me and asked me to have lunch with him. I could not turn away a free lunch. What a dilemma I was in! I was sixteen years old with no money, no job, no food, and far away from home with just my clothes and my virginity and a plan to con some guy out of his apartment.

Paul was so nice, I trusted him immediately. I invited him to come over and visit me sometime. I told him I lived in the apartment with my brother, just in case he had any crazy ideas. He did come over a few times, and we sat and watched TV and chatted about our families. He could not believe that I had gone through so much abuse. He had never met anyone like me before. We became friends. After a couple of visits, I confessed that actually I did not live with my brother. He was shocked when I revealed the truth.

He thought it was hilarious. "A little girl like you conned a guy into paying a month's rent and then locked him out? That's so funny. He didn't bother you any more after that?"

"He came back a few times, but then I threatened to call the police to report him for trying to force me to sleep with him. Danny knew I was only sixteen, so that scared him, and he hasn't come back since." When Paul left, I spent some time evaluating my situation.

I was proud of myself, but I knew that time was running out. I had only two weeks of free rent left. I had to think of something fast.

The next day, I combed the community again, looking for any kind of a job. I met a lot of people, but no one hired me. I was walking back toward the apartment when a young man stopped me and introduced himself as Dion DeMucci, the singer. I was hoping to meet Dion, so I played along.

"You do look a little like him," I said.

"That's because I *am* him," he said in a sexy voice.

"All right, then sing *The Wanderer* for me," I said. He sang it, and he even sounded a little like Dion. I thanked him for the entertainment and wished him good luck.

After leaving Dion, I decided to take a shortcut to the apartment. I was walking on one of the side streets off Whittier Boulevard when I noticed a man sitting in a car waiting for someone. I did not know that he was waiting for me.

"Hey, young lady," he shouted from his car, "come over here. I want to ask you a question." As I approached the car, he jumped out, grabbed me, and threw me onto the front seat. He put a knife at my throat with one hand and began to tear my clothes off with the other. I became hysterical. *"Please, don't hurt me! Please, don't kill me!"*

For a moment, I was a victim. Then something snapped in my brain. Perhaps it was triggered by the years of abuse I had suffered at home or simply the self-preservation instinct, but suddenly I felt a surge of power within me, and I became an unleashed tiger. I kicked and scratched and pounded in a flurry of arms and legs. My surprised assailant dropped the knife and tried to protect himself, and at the right moment I was able to reach the passenger door handle and open the door. In a matter of seconds, I was outside and running away. I could hear him swearing that he would find me and kill me, but he did not follow me. He just sat there in his car, probably licking his wounds. This time I was the victor.

Breakaway

My heart was pounding from the adrenalin rush as I ran to the safety of the apartment a couple of blocks away, looking over my shoulder now and again to see if I was being followed. I reached the apartment safely and locked the door. I took off my torn clothes and collapsed on the bed, completely exhausted from the ordeal, and fell into a deep sleep.

Unfortunately, I did not get the license plate number of the assailant's car, but I did have a good description of him to give to the police. When I woke up, the whole thing seemed like a nightmare. I reported the incident to the authorities with as much information as I could remember. They said they would keep an eye out for the offender, but there was not much hope of catching him without a license plate number.

I stayed in the apartment for two days out of fear of being seen by my attacker. My California dream was in fact becoming a nightmare. My resources were gone, and time was running out. I only had a few days until I would have to give up the apartment. Without transportation, there was little hope of my finding work. How could I survive like this? I did not know what to do. I did not want Casey, Jack, and Tonya to know that I had failed. I still had my pride and, of course, my virginity, but otherwise I was desperate.

Feeling hopeless, I was unaware that my guardian angel was looking for me. Somehow, Rachel and J.T. had got in touch with Casey and Jack and learned of my general whereabouts. They took the trouble to try to find me. They would drive up and down Whittier Boulevard from time to time, searching all the areas where they thought I might be. I was out walking along Whittier Boulevard one morning when J.T. pulled up to the curb. He jumped out of the car and gave me a big hug. I was so happy to see him! It was incredible timing. I do not know what I would have done if he had not come by just then.

We sat in his car for a while and talked, trying to catch up on the events of the past weeks. I had to confess my failure to flourish on my own. I told him everything from conning Danny to the attempted rape, including all my failed attempts to find work.

99

The confession emptied me of all my pride. The only thing left was my virginity.

"J.T.," I said, "I have to go back home. I really wanted to make it in California, but things have not worked out. Besides, I want to go home and see my family. I miss them all. I especially miss my sisters and my brother. I won't have a place to stay next week. I've completely run out of options."

J.T. was very sympathetic. "I understand, and I can help. I'm really sorry you've been through so much, Nadia. Much of it is my fault. I'm so sorry. I'll get a ticket for you on the Greyhound and send you back home." He gave me a few dollars for food and told me to stay in the apartment until he contacted me. He kept his promise. The next day, he was back with my ticket, and my California adventure was over.

When I returned home, my mother was very happy to see me. I'm sure that my father was, too, but he was not good about showing his real feelings. My siblings could not wait to hear about all my adventures, and it was especially great to see my old friends Teresa, Karen, and Donna again. I also looked forward to seeing Billy. When I returned from Beirut and saw him with another girl, I lost interest, but now I was excited to see him again. It was good to be home.

I came back a different girl, far less naive than I was before. My world was greatly enlarged by the weeks on the road with the magazine crew. Cold calling helped me to overcome my shyness. I learned how to talk confidently to complete strangers. I learned a whole lot about people, both positive and negative. I learned that I could make decisions for myself and meet new challenges to survive, even if it meant conning some guy out of his apartment! In short, I had become far more streetwise and much stronger.

I would need all the strength I could rally in the coming year. It would be one of the most difficult years of my life.

We look to the left and then to the right
And drive unguided through the night
Of darkness that enfolds the world
In constant consternation.

Crash

I THOUGHT THAT AFTER FOUR MONTHS OF BEING away, things would be different at home. I especially hoped that my father would treat me better. I reasoned that since I was gone for the summer and came back a virgin, it would show my parents that I was not a whore like they thought I was. I was mistaken.

The fall school term began, and I enrolled in the tenth grade. I dropped out of high school only three months later, but not before one of the darkest days in the history of our country.

I was in my social studies class when I heard the news over the public address system: "President John F. Kennedy has been shot." Everyone in my class was shocked. All the girls screamed when we heard the news. The whole school was in a panic at first, and then it went strangely quiet. No one spoke. No one moved. Every student and every faculty member sat in stunned silence, alone with their own thoughts. After a few minutes, the principal announced that all classes were dismissed and all students should go home immediately. Even the teachers were dismissed. I hurried home, crying the whole way and wondering what would happen to our country. My father was at work, but I found my mother in tears. We watched the news together on TV. The President was dead. It was one of the saddest days of my life.

I regretted the decision to leave school, because it was my life, my safe haven, but I had no choice. I could not continue being accused of doing things that I was not doing. If I missed my bus, my father accused me of fooling around with the boys at school, and a beating followed. I decided that I had to find a job, get a car, and leave home as soon as possible.

Autumn that year created the most beautiful multi-colored trees of gold, red, and yellow. I used the symbolism of the change in seasons to seek a change in my parents' attitude about my independence. I asked them to help me get a permit and teach me how to drive.

To my great surprise, my father agreed. "I'll buy a new car for you, Nadia, if you get a job and pay for it." I was ecstatic! I went job hunting and found one as a cashier at a local liquor store. I had to lie about my age because I was too young to sell liquor, but I needed the cash. The new cars would be out within a couple of months. I wanted an avocado green Mustang. I still could not believe my good fortune. Why was my father willing to help me get a car, even though I had to pay for it? The payments were around eighty-five dollars a month, but it was a small price to pay for my freedom.

We bought the car, but teaching me to drive was not easy. My father only had the weekends to work with me, and my lessons usually conflicted with his other interests. He did not want to miss his western shows on TV. He loved to watch *The Lone Ranger, Hopalong Cassidy, Gunsmoke, Wagon Train, Have Gun Will Travel, Bonanza,* and, most of all, the singing cowboys *Roy Rogers* and *Gene Autry.* If there was a western show on TV, my father watched it.

Breakaway

One day, out of frustration, I took the car keys without my father's permission. I was tired of begging to drive my own car. I was paying for it but never driving it. My father drove it all the time, so I took the keys and sneaked outside, got into the Mustang, and drove off. I decided to drive to Detroit to visit my aunt Grace who lived on West Grand Boulevard. I did not tell her that I was driving with only a driver's permit. She thought I had my license.

On the way, I came to a four-way stop and applied the brakes, stopping well before the intersection. Another car stopped to my left. I waited a few seconds, and the lady driver did not move. I was not sure what to do, so I accelerated and entered the intersection. Unfortunately, she decided to go forward at the same time but somewhat faster than I. In a split second, she was in front of me, and I rammed right into her car. The passenger side of her car was badly damaged. Fortunately, no one was sitting there. Neither she nor I were injured. My car's bumper was dented, but otherwise there was no damage.

Someone in the neighborhood called the police. I was a nervous wreck. I knew I was in deep trouble. I expected my father to beat me, without a doubt. Two officers arrived in a patrol car and began their routine by questioning the lady driver. When they finished with her, I was allowed to give my version of the accident.

"She saw me leave the stop sign, and then she started into the intersection. She pulled right in front of me. Shouldn't she have waited until I cleared the intersection?" I told the officers exactly what happened, right down to the last detail.

"May I see your driver's license, young lady?" the handsome officer asked.

"Well, I have a permit, not a license," I confessed reluctantly.

"Where are your parents? You're not supposed to be driving without supervision."

"My father was too busy, so I took the car myself."

"Does your father know?"

"No, he doesn't."

"We have to call him to come down here. What's his phone number?"

"Please, don't call him," I sobbed. "He'll beat me. Please don't. Can't we do this without him?"

"We have to call him. I'm very sorry. You're driving without a license. He is responsible for you. Things don't look good for you right now. You have a serious situation here. You're lucky no one was injured. What is your father's number?" The officer was kind but firm.

My father was busy watching a western on TV when he took the call. Imagine his surprise when he answered the phone and was told by the police that I was in an accident! Ten minutes later he was at the scene. I parked my car as the police officers had directed me. They parked their squad car behind me. My father parked behind them. The police told my father not to blame me. It was not entirely my fault, but I would be written up for driving without a license. My father told them that I took the keys while he was watching TV. He was not aware that I had the car until they called him about the accident.

We waited while the officer finished writing. "Mr. Habibi, here's the accident report. You'll need to call your insurance company right away, and you'll need to take care of the ticket with the court." My father took the paperwork and ordered me to follow him home. He was not happy. He drove off and left me with the police. To this day, I do not know why my father and the police officers allowed me to drive home unsupervised. At any rate, I thanked the police officers, got into the Mustang, started the engine, and put the car in gear. I was about to take off when the handsome but firm police officer tapped on my window. I kept my foot on the brake and rolled the window down halfway.

"Are you okay?" he asked.

"My father is going to beat me for this when I get home," I sobbed.

"You'll be all right. I'll call your father and warn him not to punish you for this." He was so concerned.

"Thanks," I replied, "I really appreciate it."

He walked slowly back to the squad car and took his place in the driver's seat. I noticed in my rearview mirror that the two officers were smiling about something. I released my foot off the brake and stepped on the accelerator. I was a bit nervous and pressed it too hard. It went right down to the floor and *crash*! I hit the front of the police car! Not paying attention, I had put the car in reverse! I looked at the officers again in my rearview mirror. They were looking at each other and shaking their heads. They were not smiling now.

The officer who had just been to my window got out of the patrol car and came back to me. I turned off the ignition, per his request, and rolled down the window.

"Oh, my God, officer, now my father *is* going to kill me," I wailed.

"You're right, young lady, your father is going to kill you." He repeated my sentence, but it sounded a lot worse coming from him. "Do you realize what you just did? It will cost hundreds of dollars to replace the bumper alone on the patrol car. It's ready to fall off. Plus, the headlights are hanging from the top of the bumper. The whole front end of our car is mutilated. You'll have to go to court and pay a large fine in addition to damages for the police car, and it may be a problem for you to get your license any time soon." The officer's voice was very stern. I could not believe this was the same officer who just a few minutes ago sounded so compassionate and caring.

"Oh, my God!" I cried. "Oh, my God!" It was all I could say.

"I'll need to call your father again. Please don't move," the officer demanded.

My father must have just got home when he took the officer's call to come back and get me. We had to leave the Mustang to be picked up later. There was considerable damage to the rear bumper and trunk now. At home, I nervously waited to discover my fate. My father said nothing.

Finally, he broke his silence. "Why did you take the car keys?" There was a beating in his tone.

"Because you never let me have the car, Baba. You never take me to show me how to drive it, and I'm paying for the car. You promised me the car, you make me pay for it every month, and you keep the keys! It's not fair. It's not my car. It's your car. I'm not going to pay for it if I can't learn to drive it." I started to cry. "You never let me drive the car. Keep it. I don't want it anymore."

I ran upstairs to my bedroom and sulked most of the night. I was lucky that he did not beat me, but it was because the police officer had asked him not to blame me and not to punish me. I also think he was afraid to do it, because he did not want me to tell the judge about it during my court appearance. He knew they would ask me whether he punished me or not.

I watched the calendar for my court date. I was worried about it, because I knew it would be expensive to repair the patrol car. I was also afraid the judge would give me a hard time and maybe keep me from getting my license. My prospects for freedom and independence were looking very grim.

My day in court finally arrived the last week of January. I expected the worst. My parents were angry because they had to pay the court for my fine and the city of Detroit for damages to police property. Of course, the Mustang had to be repaired as well. That would be expensive, too. My father worked hard for his money, and there was nothing to spare. My parents would have to scrimp now to take care of their budget. They did not care that I might never get my license. I had made a real mess of things.

My mother went to court with me. We had barely entered the courthouse when I heard someone calling out my name. It was the handsome police officer that wrote the accident report. He hurried down the hall toward us.

"Hello, Mrs. Habibi, how are you?"

"Okay, officer," she replied unenthusiastically.

"Where's Mr. Habibi?"

"He's at work. Thank you, officer," she replied.

"Nadia, I have a proposal for you and your mother." The officer sounded more like his compassionate self now. His eyes were very kind as he looked at me.

"What is it, sir?" I asked humbly.

"I'm going to talk to the judge and ask him to remove your case, and you won't have to appear in court."

"You can do that?" I was flabbergasted.

"Yes, but only under one condition."

"What's that?"

"If your parents will let you go out with me to dinner and a movie, I'll get everything cleared, and it will be like nothing ever happened."

I looked at my astonished mother, and she smiled back at me. She was happy to let me go to dinner and a movie with the police officer, as long as it meant that we did not have to appear in court. She agreed to let him take me out whenever he wanted to. It was far better than paying hundreds of dollars for the damages to the police car in addition to court costs. I was happy, too. I was going to dinner and a movie with a cute policeman. Of course, I did not need to give him our phone number, since he had already called it twice! He said he would call me the next week. We said goodbye and went back home to my father with the good news. He listened to our story and could hardly believe it. No fines? No court appearance? No damages? How could it be? I never saw him more relieved. I was relieved, too. Surprisingly, my father and I were happy together over something. Besides, I was hopeful again that I might get a license to drive someday.

The police officer called, and we set our date for the following Friday evening, Valentine's Day, but his date with me was not without rules. My mother and father spoke soberly to the policeman when he arrived at our house.

"Officer," my father began, but he was interrupted.

"Call me Steve, Mr. Habibi," said the officer. "I'm out of uniform now, and we're friends."

"Okay, Steve, you're a policeman, so you know about the law. You know that my daughter is a minor. She's also a virgin.

You bring her home the same way. That's all we ask. We trust you because you're a police officer, or we wouldn't let Nadia go with you." Why did he have to say that? I was so embarrassed!

"Don't worry, Mr. Habibi," he replied, "I'd never do anything to hurt Nadia or your reputation. She'll be fine. I just want her to have a good time at dinner and a movie. I'll have her home by ten o'clock."

"That's good, Steve," replied my father. "Thank you, thank you for everything. You're a good man." He reached out and shook Steve's hand.

Steve took me to dinner and a movie, both of which we thoroughly enjoyed. He brought me safely home, right on time as he promised. We never saw him again. He took care of us out of the goodness of his heart without expecting anything in return. I believe he acted out of compassion for the abusive life I had, and he wanted to bring some happiness into it for a few hours. He was indeed a good man.

On the other hand, I never received a beating for crashing the Mustang. There were certain times, for whatever reason, that my father was a good man, too.

Hope swells within our hearts and then
It ebbs away without our ken,
But still we reach to bring it near
By our imagination.

Sammy's Pizzeria

ECAUSE I DID NOT HAVE A DRIVER'S LICENSE, the insurance company refused to pay for damages to the Mustang, so I had to pay. I immediately left the liquor store to find a better paying job. I always enjoyed working, and finding work was easy, except for that August in California when I could not find a job. I had held several jobs, even before going to Lebanon, but in no case did I ever stay at one thing very long.

My first job was at White Castle, reportedly the oldest fast food chain restaurant in America. It was started in the early 1920s and was famous for its square burgers. They sold for ten cents and were advertised with the slogan "What You Crave."

There were several White Castle restaurants in the greater Detroit area. I was hired on the cleaning detail at the newest one. I was already used to cleaning before I started there because of all the cleaning I had done at home since the age of eight. I scrubbed the walls until I thought the Formica would come off, and then my skills were applied to the floors and the restrooms. Everything had to be spotless. I could deal with everything but the restrooms. They were disgusting. I left after one week.

After White Castle, I landed a couple of cashier jobs. One was at Shopper's Fair where I made a dollar and fifty cents an hour, the minimum wage. I was fifteen at the time. It was right after I came back from Lebanon. This job did not suit me either. I wanted to move around. I liked meeting all the people but not being tied to a register.

Now, two years later, seasoned by working at Blazo's and selling magazines on the road, I was working at Sammy's Pizzeria as a waitress. I really enjoyed working there. All kinds of cute guys came in, some with girlfriends and some alone. I preferred the alone kind.

I had been at Sammy's for about a month when I met my dream man. He had light brown, carmel-colored hair, green eyes, and small features accenting his handsome face. He was very cool and talked softly like Ricky Nelson. He even looked a little like him. He was a really sexy guy. I was certifiably boy crazy. I flirted with every good-looking guy that walked in, but this one was different. Mr. Cool sat in my section. I thought it was a sign from heaven.

I floated over to his booth and greeted him with a smile, "Hi, may I take your order?"

He looked at me and said, "I'd like a large pizza with pepperoni and cheese, and most of all I'd like you to join me."

"I'd love to," I replied enthusiastically, "but I can't. As you can see, I'm working. I've only been here a month, and I can't afford to get fired."

He looked at me with inviting eyes, "What time do you get off work?"

"Five o'clock," I said.

"Well, how about if I come back then and you have dinner with me?" he asked.

"Okay, that will be great." I was so excited!

Breakaway

An elderly man seated next to a gray-haired lady yelled his impatience from a booth across the restaurant: *"Hey, waitress, we're ready to order over here!"*

"I have to go, I'll see you later," I slipped away from the Nelson look-a-like and glided over to the impatient old people. My sails were full of wind. I dropped anchor to take their order, but it was too late.

Sammy was watching me flirt, and he was upset that I neglected the other patrons. At five o'clock, Sammy, a congenial, short Italian with a big, black mustache and an even bigger heart, put his arm around me and said, "You are-a nice-a girl, but too-a wild for this-a place, come-a back when-a you are-a bit-a older."

Sammy fired me right on the spot. I was shocked! "Sammy, I'll do better," I promised. I was very nervous. I had never been fired before.

"You are-a boy-a crazy. I am-a sorry. You cannot-a work-a here-a now," he repeated.

"Okay, Sammy. It's okay, I understand," I said warmly. Sammy was a nice man.

Then my handsome guy walked in, and I forgot all about Sammy. We sat in the same booth that he had earlier. He ordered a large pizza for us, and we talked for a long time. He said his name was Bobby Lee. He was from Columbus, Ohio, and had been in Detroit for only a month. He also said that I was the first girl he had met and liked. I gave him my name and a talked a little bit about my life. It was like we had known each other for a long time. He was a quiet person: gentle, charming, warm, and very easy to talk to.

We enjoyed the pizza and left Sammy's together, walking down West Vernor Highway. He pointed to his apartment building near the highway and asked me if I would like to see his place.

"No, thanks, not today, Bobby," I said. "I just met you, it's getting late, and I have to get home, or my father will be waiting for me with a belt."

"What! With a belt?" He was astonished.

"Yes. I'll tell you about that another time."

111

"When can I see you again?" he probed.

"I don't know, Bobby."

"How about giving me your phone number?" He was very persistent.

"I can't. I'm not allowed to have a boyfriend. But give me yours and I'll call you." I handed him a pencil and a piece of paper. He wrote his phone number down and hurried off. I memorized it and threw the paper away.

"Call me soon," he yelled.

I waved goodbye and headed for the bus stop.

I boarded the city bus and went straight home. I did not tell my father that I had been fired, as I believed I would find another job soon. I went hunting for work in Detroit the next day. I got hired at A&W Root Beer, a drive-in with hot dogs and hamburgers. It was at Miller Road and Vernor Highway, close to Dix Avenue. Like White Castle, A & W Root Beer restaurants had been around a long time, having got their start in Lodi, California. I was told they were the first to have drive-in, curbside service. The job was perfect for me. It was a new place where for five cents you could get a huge, frosted mug filled with root beer, and ten cents bought you one twice as large. The inch of foam on top was free.

I met the owner named Tom O'Brian. Mr. O'Brian was a pleasant Irishman, about thirty years old. He was wearing a business suit and tie, very conservative and very proper. He hired me on the spot.

"Can you start tomorrow?" he asked.

"Yes, I can," I replied enthusiastically.

"Good, be here at ten o'clock. We'll train you. Your pay will start at a dollar and fifty cents an hour, plus you'll keep all your tips. A pretty girl like you should make a lot from tips." I thought for a moment about what he said. How odd it seemed that everybody said I was pretty, but I did not feel that way myself. Nevertheless, I was very excited to be back to work after one day of unemployment!

I started work the next morning. I had a different attitude about this job. Older people came, teenagers came, everyone was friendly, and how they loved those root beer floats! My uniform was different, too. The A&W uniform was a white, short-sleeved blouse, orange and chocolate-brown striped skirt, with a two-pocket apron tied neatly around my waist to hold my order pad and pencil.

I worked at A&W for some time paying off my debt to the Mustang, but I never forgot Bobby's phone number. Even today, I remember phone numbers and addresses I had thirty years ago, and I have moved more than forty times in my life! I was a little shy about calling Bobby, but I finally got the nerve to do it. I told him where I was working, and we chatted for a few minutes. He sounded really excited to hear from me and said he would meet me for a root beer after I finished work. We had a great time together, just like the first day we met. It was nice to see him again.

Mr. O'Brian was right; I made good money from tips. I earned at least thirty to fifty dollars in tips on every shift, and every cent went to my parents, even after I finished paying for the accident. They promised me I could have some of it for clothes and shoes, but it never happened without a fight.

One day, I went to the store and bought a pair of white pants, a red and white ruffled blouse, and a pair of white shoes. I thought I would do some shopping before giving them my earnings.

When I got home, my father said, "Is this all the money?"

"Yes, Baba, that's it."

"Where's the rest of it?" he demanded. "There's only ten dollars here."

"Okay, I'll tell you. I went to the store. I bought some clothes." I showed him my new prizes. "See, just a pair of pants, a top, and matching shoes. I need clothes. I'm working every day, and I don't keep any money. I'm sixteen years old, and I don't have any nice clothes."

"Did I tell you to take the money?" he asked.

"No, Baba, you never give me money, and I can't even keep what I earn." I was livid.

My father angrily told me to take the clothes back and get a refund. I was shattered. Surprisingly, my mother stepped up and asked him to let me keep the clothes, but I was made to promise that next time I would be sure to ask him first. It took some convincing and begging from both of us to let me keep the clothes.

Grudgingly, he gave in.

I kept the clothes.

Upward, upward is our climb,
A millimeter at a time.
Imperceptibly we grow
Through strong determination.

Trapped

I WAS WORKING AND HAD A SECRET BOYFRIEND who treated me better than I had ever been treated by anyone. I had known Bobby for several months. By now we had a comfortable relationship. He knew I was a virgin, and he knew my father would kill me if I had sex with anybody before marriage, so he never tried to do anything. He was a good listener, and I really trusted him. We had a friendship. He respected me, knowing what my life was like. I felt very safe with him.

Still, I never went to his apartment, because I was afraid to. I was afraid that someone might see me go there and tell my father, even though no one knew about Bobby and me except for a few of my friends, some of whom had met him and liked him as well. Sometimes, we would all meet at Cunningham's Drug Store on Dix Avenue and Wyoming Street to eat ice cream floats and listen to the jukebox.

A lot of my favorite songs were on that jukebox. There was plenty of room at Cunningham's to dance, so we took advantage of it. We danced the calypso to songs like *Under the Boardwalk* by the Drifters. We did the locomotion as we sang along with Little Eva: "Come on, baby, do the locomotion with me," and, of course, we did the mashed potato with James Brown. We could not sit still when the Beatles sang *Twist and Shout*, and we twisted to a lot of other songs. When we got tired of dancing, we just sat and talked and listened to the jukebox in the background. Some of my other favorite songs were: *Be My Baby* (Ronettes); *I'm Leaving It Up To You* (Dale and Grace); *Oh Pretty Woman* (Roy Orbison); *My Guy* (Motown's own Mary Wells); *Chapel of Love* (Dixie Cups); *He's So Fine* (Chiffons); *Blue Velvet* (Bobby Vinton); *Walk Right In* (Rooftop Singers); and everything that Elvis sang. I memorized all his songs. What a great escape Cunningham's was for me! I still love those songs!

I had to sneak out of the house to join my friends or tell my parents that I was going to visit my cousin on the next street. Sometimes I got away with it, and sometimes I got caught. One day, I got caught while walking with my friends. My father was driving his new Lincoln Mercury. He saw me and stopped his car in the middle of the street. He jumped out, ran over to me, grabbed my long hair, and literally dragged me to the car in front of all my friends. They were in shock. They called him names, yelling, "*Leave her alone!*" He pushed me onto the front seat, closed the car door, and went after my friends who all took off as fast as they could. He wanted to scare them, and he certainly did. Then he got into the car and drove home. He was full of rage. I knew what was coming next.

He pulled up into our driveway, slammed on the brakes, grabbed me by the arm, and dragged me into the house.

"How many times do I have to tell you not to go with boys? How many times do I have to tell you not to go with Teresa? How many times?" he ranted. He removed his belt and began to beat me with it. I cowered and cried for him to stop, doing my best to protect my head and face with my hands and arms, but he continued in a fit of anger. After a lashing with the belt, he proceeded to beat me with his fists until he knocked me to the floor. Then he kicked me until I could not get up. Limp and exhausted, I just lay on the floor and sobbed for a long time until I gained the strength to move. I struggled up the stairs to my bedroom, collapsed on the bed, and went to sleep.

Saturday came, and it was my day off. I called Bobby and arranged to meet him at Sammy's for a soda. We had our soda and talked about what had happened to me that week. He was very sympathetic. Bobby said he was thinking about going back to Columbus for a while, but he would return. His uncle had called him asking for help with some business planning.

"Hey, you've never seen my apartment," he said casually. "Come on, nobody will see you, I promise. Besides, I'm leaving soon, and I want you to see my pad. Just come for a few minutes, and go home whenever you want. I'll make popcorn for us, and we can watch TV a little. What do you think? C'mon, sweetie, you trust me don't you?" He was so persuasive.

"Yes, Bobby, I trust you. I'll stay for half an hour, and then I'll have to leave."

We walked the short distance to his apartment. I had a strange feeling when he opened the door. I did not know why, but in retrospect, his apartment was situated a lot like my grandfather's room—the long stairs, the second floor, the retail shops below. We climbed the stairs and stepped into the apartment. It was very small. There was a tiny kitchen, a bathroom, and a bed right in the middle of the shoebox-sized living room. His TV was on a stand near the bed. There was no sofa or anywhere else to sit.

"Where would you like to sit?" he asked with a smile.

"I'll sit on the floor, thanks," I replied, thinking it was safer than the bed.

He went to the kitchen, made popcorn, and told me how happy he was that I had finally come over.

"See, nobody knows. It's just you and me here," he said reassuringly.

He turned the TV on, and we ate popcorn.

"Nadia, you're so sweet, so innocent, and so beautiful," he said. "I'm so glad you're here with me." He put his arm around me while I was sipping my Coke.

I suddenly felt uneasy, almost like I was having a flashback. Something was not right. I began to perspire. My heart started to race, and I felt like running. Before I could move, Bobby was forcing himself on me, kissing me. In a few heartbeats, he had pinned me down flat on the floor. I struggled to get free, but he was much too strong. In a few seconds it was all over. He took his pleasure and handed me a death sentence. He held my mouth shut and told me not to scream, as he continued to hold me down.

"I won't hurt you, Nadia. I promise. I love you," he lied.

"*Get off me! Let me up, Bobby!*" My muffled voice could hardly be heard through his hand. He saw the terror on my face and released me.

I jumped up and screamed at him. "*Oh, my God! Why did you do that? Are you crazy? Oh, my God, Bobby, what am I going to do now? Why did you rape me? I trusted you. If my father finds out, he'll kill me. Don't you understand what you have done to me? My father will come here and kill you, too! Why did you rape me?*" I choked on the sound of the word. *Rape!* It seemed foreign to me as it echoed through my mind. *Rape! Rape! Rape!* How could this happen to me? I could barely see through my burning tears. I could hear my pulse pounding in my head.

Bobby said nothing.

I ran down the stairs and up the street like a gazelle chased by a leopard. I hated myself. I hated Bobby. I was hysterical. I could not stop crying, but I needed to regain my composure. I had to act like nothing happened. No one must know. My white blouse was wrinkled, and my peacock blue skirt looked like it had never been ironed. I kept running, running with hot breath, running and hoping that nobody I knew would see me. No one could see how disheveled I looked. I ran all the way home. Almost ready to collapse, I opened the side door quietly and ran downstairs to the basement where I undressed and took a shower. I had to hurry. I was not sure where everyone was. They would wonder why I was taking a shower in the middle of the day. Were they upstairs or outside? Were they looking for me now? I toweled myself dry, found some clothes in the laundry basket, and dressed quickly. My hair was long down to my waist. It was a complete mess. I brushed it as best I could. If I had a scissors at that moment, I would have cut it all off. I was so angry. So humiliated. So exhausted.

No one was upstairs, so I went outside. What a relief! My aunt and uncle were sitting with my parents at the picnic table eating fresh fruit and playing cards. We had a big back yard. It was at least half an acre. The yard was actually comprised of two lots. The house was situated in the center, straddling the two. The unattached garage was located behind the house on one side. The picnic table was located on the far side of the lot opposite the garage. I slipped unseen behind the garage and went back into the house. Fortunately, even my siblings were not around. I went to my room and isolated myself for the rest of the day. I needed to hide. I felt like hiding forever.

I acted like everything was all right at dinner that evening, but I felt sick to my stomach and still dirty even after the shower, not physically dirty, but crawly with an intangible dirt that was far worse. It was very difficult to act normal, but I did it. I deserved an Oscar for that performance. I knew that if my parents discovered what had happened, it would be over for me. No question about it.

At the same time, I wanted Bobby to pay for what he did, but I could not call the police. I was trapped. I was not even supposed to have a boyfriend, let alone go to his apartment. I did everything I should not have done. How stupid was that! It would not matter that I was raped. I lost my virginity in a selfish and meaningless act of violence. The treasure I had protected so carefully was gone. My uniqueness was gone. What would happen to me now? I cannot say how relieved I was when it finally came time to go to bed.

The next day I saw my friend, Teresa, and told her what happened to me.

She was dumbfounded. "Nadia, I can't believe he did that to you, you poor thing. Did you call the police?"

"No, I can't. My father will kill me if he finds out that I went to a boy's apartment and got raped." I was trembling so badly that Teresa put her arm around me.

"How old is Bobby?" she asked.

"He's twenty."

"He can go to jail. He raped a minor. You're only seventeen," she explained.

"Well, I can't call the police. I don't want my father to kill me." I was trying to be brave, but I was terrified inside.

"You're right," Teresa said. "Maybe the guys can go and see Bobby and find out why he did this to you."

"I was a virgin, Teresa, he wanted to be the first one. I'm so scared. I feel that people are watching me. I feel that everyone knows I was raped. What am I going to do?" I was crying now full force.

"Let's hope you don't get pregnant," Teresa remarked sadly.

I stopped crying instantly. *"What did you say?"*

"I said, let's hope you don't get pregnant," she repeated.

"Oh, my God! Oh, my God! Do you think so? Will I get pregnant? I just got raped. Why would I get pregnant?"

"Nadia, if he finished inside of you, you might get pregnant. Did he take it out or stay inside of you?"

"I don't know, Teresa. I can't remember. It all happened so fast. I was sitting on the floor, and then I was pinned flat to the floor with my skirt covering my face. That's all I know. I remember getting kind of dizzy. Then my mind went numb. It's almost like my body was there but my mind left it, like I flew away from it. It was all a blur. It happened so fast. I don't know, Teresa, I really don't know how it happened. I just know it did. I feel so horrible. My father doesn't have to kill me. I feel dead already."

Teresa kept her arm around me. We walked in silence for a long while, just walking, not going anywhere in particular. I could not speak. I was too drained. From time to time, Teresa would squeeze me and interrupt our silence to say softly, "Nadia, you poor thing, you poor thing. I wish there was something I could do."

Breakaway

To what great purpose is a tree,
We ask ourselves in maturity—
To stand and wait while others serve
And bear humiliation?

Let Her Die

FOUR WEEKS PASSED, AND MY MOTHER WAS yelling at me for not cleaning the kitchen floor on my hands and knees. I had used a mop instead. My knees were too sore. I had to clean the linoleum floors three times a week, wash the clothes once a week, hang them outside, take them down, and fold or hang each piece. I also had to make lunches for my siblings every day and help cook the evening meal. These were all chores I had been doing since the age of eight.

"I have no life," I yelled back at my mother. Suddenly, I felt feverish and nauseous. I ran to the bathroom and vomited.

"*Yaaaaa*, Nadia, why did you vomit?" my mother asked sternly.

"I don't know. You made me nervous. I guess that's why."

"I'm taking you to the doctor to see why you're sick," she said firmly.

"I don't need to go the doctor, I'll be all right."

I had no clue why I vomited. I did not think anything of it. I had no idea what brought on those symptoms, but my mother was obviously suspicious.

"Maybe I have the flu," I said.

She took me to see her doctor. He greeted me cheerfully and asked my mother if she would please wait outside the room while he examined me. When he finished the exam, the doctor's expression became very serious.

"Nadia," he said soberly, "I'm so sorry to tell you that you're four weeks pregnant."

My heart leaped into my throat, and I almost fainted. "Oh, my God! Are you sure? Please don't tell my mother," I pleaded. "My parents will kill me. Please, Dr. Greenfield."

He placed his hand on my shoulder, "I have to tell her. It's the law. You're a minor. I could lose my license if I don't tell her. I'm so sorry, Nadia."

"But Dr. Greenfield, I got raped. It wasn't my fault. There was nothing I could do. He forced me." I began to cry loudly.

"I understand," he said sympathetically. "Don't cry."

My mother heard me crying and rushed into the room. "What's the matter, Nadia, why are you crying?" she demanded.

"Mrs. Habibi," the doctor said, "I have bad news for you. Your daughter is four weeks pregnant."

"*Yeeeeeeeeeeee! Yeeeeeeeeeee! Ya-Allah!*" She screamed hysterically. Her face went pale. I thought she was going to collapse. She stared blankly at the doctor for a moment. Then she began to pull her hair and scream obscenities at me, calling me a whore and an f---ing bitch.

Dr. Greenfield kindly intervened. "Please, Mrs. Habibi, it's not your daughter's fault. She was raped. She was afraid to tell you. Now, calm down, go home, talk things over, and let me know how she's doing. Come back and see me in three months. Nadia can have the baby and put it up for adoption or, of course, you can keep the baby. Abortion is not an option. It's against the law. It's a federal crime."

"*Yeeeeeeeeeeeeeee*," my mother screamed again and then went strangely silent.

After a few moments in which she seemed to drift far away in her thoughts, she gathered herself enough to thank the doctor. Then she grabbed me by the hand and literally dragged me out to the car. My mother is a tiny lady, only five feet tall, but she was tough, very tough when she was young. She had to be. She took more than her share of beatings from my father as well. Now she drove in silence for the longest time. I was quiet, too, waiting for the dam to burst. It certainly did after we had driven a couple of miles, as she screamed at me in Arabic, "What did you do? You whore! You're nothing but an f---ing whore! We didn't raise a slut! All those beatings your father gave you were for nothing. What will people say?"

"Mama, I didn't *do* anything," I said timidly. "I got raped. It happened so fast. I couldn't do anything about it. He forced himself on me. I didn't tell you because I didn't want you and Baba to kill me. I would have called the police, but I was afraid of you and Baba. I didn't think you'd believe me." I tried to speak calmly, but my voice was trembling.

"Where does that son of a bitch live?" she asked angrily.

I told her about Bobby's apartment. She wanted to go there immediately. We did, but he was gone. The apartment was vacated. He left knowing he would be arrested for raping a minor, or maybe he knew my father would come to kill him.

"Why did you go to his apartment?"

"I trusted Bobby," I tried to explain. "You don't let me date, so I don't know when someone is lying to me. I don't know anything about sex and babies. I don't know anything about life. I'm nothing to you and Baba. I'm just a stupid, dumb whore. That's what you always call me. Now I'm a stupid, dumb, pregnant whore. I got raped because I don't know anything about life."

She listened but did not say anything, so I continued. "I'm only a servant, cleaning, cooking, and working. I have no life. Just kill me and get it over with."

I really did not care anymore. I was tired of life, tired of being beaten by my father, tired of being a prisoner with endless rules, tired of not having control of my own life, tired of always being wrong. Now I had reached the end of the road. Not knowing what to do and what not to do, never able to do the right thing, my broken spirit collapsed. We drove in silence the rest of the way home.

Before we got out of the car, my mother warned me not to say anything at all to anyone about my being pregnant. She promised not to tell my father. She said that if he found out, he would kill both of us. I had no doubt that she was right. I certainly would not tell him.

Once inside the house, my mother immediately called a female relative of hers to get some advice. Apparently, this person was very streetwise and had a lot of connections that my mother would never have dreamed of. My mother told her in detail about my situation. Then she was silent, as she listened to what the other person was saying. My mother only said, "Okay," at the end of the call.

The next morning, a lady, a close relative to whom I'll give the name Adara (the meaning of which is *virgin*), arrived at our house at nine o'clock. She talked with my mother through the screen door. She said she wanted us to go with her to an undisclosed location. I sensed that we were living out the plan Adara had discussed with my mother on the phone, but I did not care. However, it was clear that I was the only one in the car who did not know where we were headed or why we were going there. The two ladies sat in the front seat, while I sat like a prisoner in the back.

We drove to an old suburb in Detroit, somewhere near Eight Mile Road. The houses were of the kind so often seen in certain areas of Detroit: small, one-story bungalows with basements, dwarfed by century-old trees lining the streets. Adara found the address she was looking for and parked in the driveway of the most rundown house in the neighborhood. We got out of the car and went to the door.

"What's going on?" I asked. Adara and my mother did not respond. Instead, they banged on the front door, and a little Mexican lady about sixty years old appeared. The door creaked as she opened it.

"*Bienvenidos, mi casa su casa*," she said in a welcoming voice that was as sweet as honey. She had salt and pepper hair, no makeup, and weary eyes. She looked tired and ragged. Her clothes were unkempt and soiled. I noticed a few, small spots of dried blood on the front of her dress.

"What are we doing here?" I asked again.

"Honey, my name Sylvia," she said in broken English. "I help you."

"What do you mean, help me?" I looked again at the blood on Sylvia's dress. Were they planning to kill me now? Were my mother and Adara planning to keep their hands clean by hiring this stranger to do their deed? No one would suspect a little, old Mexican lady who was completely unknown to our family. They could dispose of me and no one would ever find me. The police would never have a clue. I would be dead in a few minutes, and my blood would be on Sylvia's dress, too. My mind was racing. I wondered if they would cut me up and put me in the basement furnace. A black cloud of doom hung over me. Like a hunted deer, I smelled danger and knew that I must run.

But escape was impossible. My mother took one of my arms, and Adara took the other. Sylvia escorted us down to her dingy, cobweb-filled basement. It was gray and dark and dusty and completely void of furniture except for an old, rusty dinette table, and, of course, the large coal or wood-burning furnace. It was obviously not a place that was lived in. It looked more like a dungeon or a torture chamber—a place of death.

They led me to the table with the Formica top, just to the right of the staircase. Sylvia told me to sit on it and relax. Adara maintained her grip on my arm, as Sylvia took my mother aside and spoke to her in a quiet voice. This was my chance to run, if only I could break free from Adara, but I was paralyzed with fear, unable to move, like the proverbial deer in the headlights.

With her broken English, I could not make out what Sylvia was saying, but my mother apparently agreed as she nodded her head. When they finished the conference, Sylvia busied herself with something behind me, and my mother returned to me, taking the side opposite Adara. Both women held my arms firmly as though they knew I would try to run away.

Sylvia's voice took my breath away. "What we do could kill her," she said matter-of-factly.

"Let her die." It was my mother's voice, cold and cruel, completely devoid of human emotion. I immediately broke into a cold sweat, trembling with fear. My mouth was as dry as the years of dust in the dirty basement where I was to be killed. I could not speak.

"Okay, Mrs., up to you," replied Sylvia coldly. "First give me the three hundred dollars, and I do it."

My mother calmly took three one-hundred-dollar bills from her pocket with her free hand and gave them to Sylvia. She then held my hand. Her hand was as hard as steel and ice cold, like a vice. There was no feeling there. It was not the hand of love. Not even a human hand.

Sylvia finished her preparations and came over to me. She had a dirty, old, green, garden hose in one hand and a butcher knife in the other. I stared at her in horror. She stood in front of me for what seemed like an eternity. Finally, she cut a section about four inches long from the hose and told me to lie down flat on my back. My mother and Adara forced me into the desired position. I could no longer see Sylvia. I heard the hose drop to the floor. That meant Sylvia still had the knife in her hand, but I could not see what she was doing with it.

"*What are you doing?*" I finally screamed. "*Mama, help me! Please, help me! Adara, help me! Don't hurt me! Don't kill me!*"

"Everything is going to be all right," my mother said icily. "Shut up and do what she tells you, or I'll kill you myself right now." She glanced at the knife and then at Adara and then at me. Four hands now tightened even more to hold me down.

"Yes, Mama," I whimpered, fully expecting those to be my last words. I heard metal on metal as Sylvia touched the knife to the table.

Then, in what seemed like one motion, Sylvia pulled my skirt up, pulled my panties off, and forced the four inches of rubber hose as far as she could inside my vagina. Instinctively, I screamed at the top of my lungs, like a wounded animal, writhing in pain. My mother and Adara added their combined weight to hold me down. I was nothing more than a piece of meat to them, like a side of beef on a butcher block. "*Oh, God! Please let me die! Please let me die!*" I screamed with all my might. There was no one to help, no one who cared, no response. Why were they doing this to me?

"Okay, Mrs., I finish. You go now. *Gracias,*" Sylvia's words were engraved on my heart, never to be forgotten.

Sylvia led us out and helped Adara and my mother put me in the back seat of the car. I did not care where they took me next. The pain was excruciating. I felt sick to my stomach. I curled up into a fetal position. I was sobbing and begging to die. I remembered the blood on Sylvia's dress. I knew that my blood was now mixed with the blood of other girls who must have been to Sylvia's basement. "Oh, God," I repeated to myself, "Please let me die! Why is this happening to me? Please, God! Please let me die!"

My mother's voice etched an unforgettable message on my mind as she issued an ultimatum. The voice was as cold as the Arctic winter. "If you tell anyone about this, it's over for you, Nadia, do you understand?"

I did not reply. I was already dead.

Dead people do not talk. I told no one. A week passed, and I felt very sick. I had a fever, and I looked very yellow. My cousin Marilee came over, since she had not heard from me.

"Hi, Nadia, are you okay? What's the matter with you? You look so pale," she said as she touched my forehead. "You're burning up with a fever. What's happening here? How come you're sick and no one is taking care of you?"

"Marilee," I pleaded, "please don't ask any questions."

"What do you mean, don't ask any questions? What's wrong with you? What have they done to you?" She would not give up.

"Please, Marilee, please don't go on."

"I don't like this," she said, her voice filled with fear. "I'm taking you to the doctor."

"No, Marilee, you can't. Please don't. They'll kill me."

She grabbed me by the arm and pulled me outside and into her car. She screeched out of the driveway and sped off. "Nadia, I won't let anyone hurt you," she said firmly. "You're going to the doctor. What did they do to you?"

"Marilee, promise not to say anything."

"I promise," she said.

"I'm pregnant. I was raped. They put a rubber hose in me about a week ago." I told her about the trip to Sylvia's basement.

"*Oh, my God, Nadia! You're going to die if I don't get you to the doctor right now.*" She was screaming. Her face was red with anger and tears were rolling down her cheeks. She stepped on the accelerator, and the car lurched forward. No ambulance could have taken me faster.

She took me to a doctor she knew well. He examined me immediately and removed the rubber hose.

"You're a lucky young lady," he said. "In a few hours, you could have died. You have a serious infection throughout your body. The hose wasn't sterile." I cried and cried and cried some more. Marilee was crying, too, and still furious. The doctor was livid that someone would do such a thing to me.

"Your fetus may not make it," he said. "You're about five weeks pregnant."

"Yes, I know, Dr. Chase."

"Who did this to you?"

"A Mexican lady." I did not dare to tell him about Adara and my mother.

"You'll probably miscarry because of the infection," he continued. "Now, I need all the information you can give me: who, what, when, where, why, how—everything in detail. I have to notify the FBI and make a police report. There will be an investigation."

"Oh, no, Dr. Chase. Please don't do that," I begged.

"It's the law," he replied firmly.

"We'll both be killed if anyone finds out. You know our culture, Dr. Chase," Marilee pleaded. "Please don't call them. Please don't make a report."

"I could lose my license if I don't," he replied sternly. He looked at both of us for a long time and then suddenly and mercifully changed his mind. "Well, all right," he sighed. "I won't make the report this time, but no one can ever know that I saw you. Is that clear?"

"Oh, yes, Dr. Chase, thank you so much. You just saved our lives." It was Marilee's voice, but I could not have agreed more. Both of our lives were in jeopardy.

The doctor gave me a penicillin shot and some other medicine and sent us on our way.

Marilee thought it would be best if I stayed with her for a while. She wanted me to be safe. She was my angel, my protector. She also knew what was going to happen with the fetus, but she said nothing to me about it. I agreed to stay with her. We both knew it was not going to be easy.

We called my parents to tell them about the doctor visit and that I was not coming back home. My mother begged me to return, stating that she was three months pregnant herself and needed my help. Her pleading went unheeded. My cousin did not back down. Marilee yelled into the phone, *"No! Absolutely not! Nadia could have died! She's staying with me!"*

Some lovers pass and carve their names,
And children stop to do the same.
How insignificant life seems—
Of worth a violation.

Dragnet

I T WAS NOT THE FIRST TIME I WAS RESCUED BY
my cousin Marilee. At the age of fifteen, I was shipped off
to Lebanon to marry my cousin. Having refused, my life
was miserable when I returned to America. My father was beating
me routinely for one thing or another, so I lived with her for a few
days from time to time.

On one of those occasions, we were window-shopping
along Vernor Highway when six teenage boys came cruising by
and honked at us. Marilee stood at the street corner and waved at
them. They looked back and waved wildly. What was she doing?
She was acting like she wanted to be picked up, but she was
married and had a baby girl. What was she up to?

"Nadia, watch this," she said.

The guys stopped and circled back. Marilee and I were
waiting for them. They pulled slowly toward the curb where we
were standing. They had rolled their windows down and were

whistling their heads off. When they were almost stopped in front of us, Marilee suddenly turned away from them and made a motion with her hand toward her mouth. She timed it perfectly. When she turned around, the boys were just stopping and going crazy. She opened her mouth wide and gave them a big smile. "Hi there, sweeties, wanna take me for a ride?" The boys looked like they had been hosed with ice water. The car careened down the street, leaving black tire tracks for a hundred feet. Marilee doubled over with laughter.

"What happened, Marilee? What did you do?"

She could not answer. She was laughing too hard. She made the same big smile at me, but she had no teeth! Her false teeth were in her hand! We laughed so hard we almost peed our pants. I still laugh when I think of that scene! It was one of the highlights of my fifteenth year.

Now my cousin had saved me again. I was glad to be with her, but I felt guilty for not being with my mother, especially since she was pregnant and crying over me. I wanted to believe that she really loved me and wanted me around, but deep in my heart I felt that she was manipulating me, trying again to control me. I knew that she was stressed out about me not living at home, not knowing what I was doing or where I was going. She did not trust Marilee. I did not feel good about the whole situation, and I was physically and mentally drained.

Marilee and I were sitting in the living room discussing my mother's situation when I had an urge to go and release my bladder again; it seemed like maybe the hundredth time. Dr. Chase had told me to drink a lot of water so I could stay hydrated, and I took him quite literally.

"Marilee, Marilee, hurry," I screamed from the bathroom.

"What's wrong, Nadia? What's going on?"

"Something fell out of my vagina! I'm bleeding! I'm bleeding to death!"

Marilee appeared in a split second. She looked where I was pointing in the toilet. "It's a blood clot," she said.

Suddenly, I had a huge cramp and sat on the toilet again. A clot the size of a grapefruit came out with pain that I cannot describe. Marilee said clots were normal in a miscarriage, but she decided to call the ambulance anyway. I was rushed to the nearest hospital.

By the time they admitted me at the emergency room, I was feeling faint. I had already lost quite a lot of blood. I was still in great pain. It hurt so badly I could hardly breathe.

"What's happening to me?" I asked the nurse. "Did I lose the baby?"

"Not yet, Nadia. We're going to give you pain shots now and a sedative to calm you down." She was very compassionate.

I was screaming my lungs out. I was in so much pain I did not care about bothering any of the other patients. I could not think of anything or anyone; the pain took over completely. The hospital staff did not seem concerned about my screaming. They had other things on their minds. They knew right away that I had been the victim of an illegal abortion. They were concerned about controlling the infection in my body, having recognized it as a life-threatening condition. Without telling me and without hesitation, they immediately notified the FBI.

After several hours in the emergency room, I was moved to a private room. I continued to cry and scream. The pain medication was not giving me relief. The agony seemed endless. It was unbearable. All I could do was call out to God for help. I really thought I was going to die.

I was lying there in utter exhaustion when I doubled up from a cramp that took my breath away. Then an enormous blood clot about the size of a toy football came out of me. The attending nurse heard my screams and came running into the room. She saw immediately that it was the fetus.

"I'm sorry, hon," she said. "I'm so sorry. You've lost the baby. There's nothing I can do."

I looked at the fetus. The baby's body was recognizable with its head and limbs already taking shape. I went ballistic. My baby was dead. I did not think about being raped. I just cried out,

"Is that my baby? Is that my baby?" I kept staring at the fetus. I was panting like a thirsty animal, crouching on the bed, screaming, "*My baby, my baby, my baby is dead!*"

The nurse was very compassionate and kind. She put her arms around me and gave me a big hug. Tears welled up in her eyes. She was a great person with a big heart. I could feel a wave of love from her. "It's okay," she said, "You're going to be all right now. It's over, sweetheart. Just relax and try to get some rest."

It was about ten thirty at night when the nurse left the room. Completely drained emotionally and physically, I fell into a deep sleep after being sedated one more time.

When I woke the next morning, two men dressed in dark suits were waiting in my room. They were like giants, and they looked very stern. They stood beside my bed like trees. Who were these men?

"Hello, are you Nadia?" the taller one asked.

"Yes, sir, who are you?"

"I'm Agent Tom Dickinson." The voice was not threatening but firm. "My partner here is Agent Bill Harris. We're from the Federal Bureau of Investigation, the FBI. The hospital informed us that you have had an abortion. Abortion is against the law. Did you have an abortion? You can tell us. We're not going to hurt you."

"Yes," I said, "but not by choice. I was forced to do it."

"Tell us the story right from the beginning. We have a job to do now, and we need your help. Tell us all the details you can."

I told them the whole story from beginning to end. They were astounded. I explained that it was shameful in my culture for a girl to lose her virginity before marriage. It was even worse to get pregnant out of wedlock, even in the case of rape. An abortion would save my parents from being dishonored and shamed, even if it meant that their eldest daughter died in the process. They said they did not understand my culture, but they would keep trying. Anyway, they needed my help.

"Where's the house you were taken to? What's the name of the street? Can you tell us the address? What's the woman's name? Who took you there?" They questioned me very thoroughly until I was too tired to go on.

I answered their questions one by one as accurately as I could. I remembered the street and the address, and I described the house and the neighborhood in detail. I told them it was near Eight Mile Road, and the lady's name was Sylvia.

"What's going to happen?" I asked.

"We're going to investigate using all the information you've given us, and we'll come back and talk to you again." They were very sympathetic and amazed that my family had put me through such a terrible ordeal just to save face.

"Thank you," I said with a worried look.

"It'll be all right," they assured me. "Get your rest. We'll be back."

The FBI agents were back at my bedside in two days. They arrived early in the afternoon, just before I was to be released from the hospital.

"Good afternoon, Nadia," they greeted me cordially. "We have some good news for you. We have arrested Sylvia Gonzalez. She'll never perform another abortion. Now, you need to sign these papers."

"Why? What papers?"

"Your signature on these papers will put Adara and your mother behind bars for a few years. They are accessories in this crime. They took you and held you against your will. In the eyes of the law, they took part in killing your baby, and they almost killed you." Agent Dickinson put the papers in front of me and handed me a pen.

"How many years will they be in jail?"

"Twenty years at the most."

"Oh, my God! I can't put them away for twenty years! What about Adara's children? What about my brothers and sisters? What will happen to them?"

"They may all go to foster homes. It's up to the courts."

"What are foster homes? I've never heard of that!"

"Different families that have strong relationships or couples who can't have children of their own work for the state. They temporarily take care of children who are abused or orphaned. The children are given a good home. In this case, the foster families will give them love and whatever else they need until the parents are out of jail. Then the families can be reunited. Foster homes are safe havens for children who otherwise might be in harm's way. Don't worry, they'll be all right."

"But in twenty years they won't be children anymore," I countered. "How can I separate the children from each other? They didn't do anything wrong. I can't do that!"

I explained to the agents that I did not hate Adara and my mother. I just wanted to have a normal life. Knowing what I had been through, they were surprised that I would not prosecute.

"We may not be able to keep Sylvia in prison unless you sign the complaint against Adara and your mother," they explained.

"I'm sorry," I replied, "I just can't do it." I felt bad for them because I knew they wanted justice for me. They really wanted me to sign the papers. They were good men. I wondered if they had daughters of their own. How would their daughters be treated if they were raped? I was sure that they would have treated their daughters exactly the way they did me, with compassion and kindness.

As the two men prepared to leave, Agent Dickinson paused at the door and looked back at me.

"Nadia," he began.

"Yes, sir?"

"Nadia, your parents have no idea how lucky they are to have you. Most of the victims we talk to would be more than willing to prosecute someone if they had been treated as badly as you have. I'd like to talk to your parents and tell them how lucky they are."

"It wouldn't make a difference," I replied, "but thank you for understanding."

"Goodbye, and good luck, Nadia. We may have to keep in touch with you if more questions come up."

I gave them my cousin Marilee's phone number and said goodbye.

I have often thought about my decision not to sign the FBI papers. My refusal to sign had a profound impact on people close to me. How very different life would have been for all the children involved if I had agreed to sign! One small act had enormous consequences. It had a huge effect on me, too.

It was a sign of mercy carved on the tree of my life. I do not know how I had the wisdom or strength to do it at the time. It would have been so easy to be bitter. Now, I know that mercy is a gift from God. People who have passed through my life have said that it is one of my character traits. It is true, and by showing mercy I have been blessed also. It has brought me favor. As it is written in the Book of Proverbs: "Do not let mercy and truth leave you. Fasten them around your neck. Write them on the tablet of your heart. Then you will find favor and much success in the sight of God and humanity."

Breakaway

We finally come to realize,
To reach our dreams and other highs,
We cannot do so on our own
Without regeneration.

Amazing Grace

I CHECKED OUT OF THE HOSPITAL ON WEDNESDAY and returned to Marilee's. Cousin Marilee's life seemed to be going well. Her beautiful daughter was several months old, and her husband, Butch, a redhead from Tennessee, was a very nice, quiet guy. My cousin was the talker in the family. Marilee was a tall, thin, aggressive, and confident person. She feared no one. But, as I have already said, her sense of humor was unique and her laughter contagious. She was a comedian most of the time. She made me laugh so much my sides and face would ache. Her laughter was the best medicine I could have taken to relieve my pain. I really enjoyed staying with her, but I was not aware that she used humor to mask her own pain. She did not tell me that her marriage was falling apart.

Life may take an unusual turn when you least expect it. The days immediately following my release from the hospital were uneventful. Marilee and I just talked about little things. But something very extraordinary happened on Sunday. I went to church. Marilee's sister, Ginger, and Aunt Grace picked me up Sunday morning around nine o'clock. Aunt Grace was born in Kentucky. She had married my uncle Fareed, my father's brother. Marilee and Ginger were his children. Aunt Grace was a devout Christian, but Fareed never attended church. He was involved somehow in some shady dealings, perhaps with organized crime, and it eventually cost him his life. A bomb planted in his car exploded when he opened the door, and he died instantly.

I had been to the mosque, but I had never seen the inside of a church building, especially one like Temple Baptist Church where four thousand people assembled at one time. I was a little nervous about going, but I went because my aunt was such a loving and caring person. She always said that she loved Jesus, and she wanted me to love him, too. I did not understand what she was talking about. I thought Jesus was a Jewish prophet who died two thousand years ago. My family never talked against Jewish people. They were our neighbors and friends. If Jesus was a Jew, it was all right with me. I loved Jewish people. I thought that meant I loved Jesus already. But Aunt Grace had something more in mind.

The congregation at Temple Baptist greeted me with a friendliness I had never encountered before. Everyone seemed so happy, so loving, and so kind. I was amazed. Was I on another planet? I had never seen so much love in people.

When the congregation was seated, the service began with a lot of singing. I did not know any of the songs, of course, but I noticed everyone around me was enjoying the music. People were singing in harmony, and some were clapping their hands enthusiastically. That was a new experience for me, too, but it did not make me uncomfortable.

After the singing, one of the assistant pastors read through the list of meetings scheduled for the week. There were a lot of things to do. Then some baskets were passed around to collect money. We were told that some of the money would go for salaries, some would go to missionaries around the world, and some would go to help the poor. I noticed that the amount of money collected the previous week was written in the bulletin we received at the door. I liked that. I was happy to see that people cared enough to give money to people they did not even know. How incredible was that! People took their hard-earned money and gave it away, not because they were forced to do it like I was, not because some higher power like the government legislated it, but because they simply loved people and wanted to help. Wow!

Finally, it was time for the sermon. The preacher's name was Dr. Vic. He was an elderly gentleman, at least seventy years old, and he was a very good speaker. I listened intently to what he said. I wanted to be loved, and I wanted to love people the way these people did.

I do not remember the title of Dr. Vic's sermon that day. I only recall that it was a simple message about the Gospel. Dr. Vic explained that the Gospel means "good news." There was very little good news in my life, so my ears were ready to hear. He said that the Gospel is good news because it brings hope to those who have no hope. He was talking to me. He said that it brings about change. I wanted change. He went on to list several other things that the Gospel does. I never missed a beat. I wanted everything he was talking about because I had none of it in my life. I was empty. As Dr. Vic was talking, I began to ask myself, "What exactly is the Gospel he's talking about?"

It was almost as though Dr. Vic had read my mind. It seemed that he was speaking directly to me from that point on. Dr. Vic exuded kindness and love as he explained the Gospel.

"Dear people," he said, "God has a plan for your life. Have you been struggling through life? Is your heart burdened? Do you feel out of control? Do feel like a prisoner? Would you like to be free?"

I began to feel a lump in my throat. He was describing me perfectly. Dr. Vic continued:

"God's plan is simply this: He loves you! I say again: He loves you! Here's how he loves you. All of us are like sheep that get lost. He is the Good Shepherd. A good shepherd looks for the lost sheep until he finds it. Then he brings it back to the fold where he feeds it, heals it, strengthens it, and protects it. Are you lost? God is the Good Shepherd. He is looking for you today. His sheep know his voice and come to him when he calls. Are you hungry or thirsty, in need of sustenance? Are you broken, in need of healing? Are you weak, in need of strengthening? Are you besieged, in need of protection? The Good Shepherd is calling you. Will you listen to His voice? Will you come to him now?"

"Yes," I said to myself, "if God says anything to me, I'll listen."

"Here's why you should listen," continued Dr. Vic. "God loves you because you're special. He knows what you are. He also knows what you can become. Only God knows the future. He has not left you alone. He has given you an example. That example is his Son, Jesus Christ. He sent his Son into the world, not to condemn the world, but that the world might be saved through him: 'For God so loved the world that he gave his only begotten Son, so that whoever believes in Him shall not perish, but shall have everlasting life.' That is what the Bible promises.

"Can you imagine that kind of love? Can you imagine such a gift? Jesus died for your sins, died in your place, and rose again to give you eternal life. That is good news. You can be free from your sins. You can be free to live your life according to God's plan. You can have a happy life here and now, and the Gospel promises you eternal life. You don't need to feel like a prisoner. There is hope for you. Will you accept Jesus as your personal savior today? Will you make him Lord of your life? Will you let him guide you? The Scripture says in another place: 'If we confess our sins, he is faithful and just to forgive us our sins and to cleanse us from all unrighteousness.'

"Think of Jesus standing and knocking at your door. Will you let him in? If you confess your sins and believe that God raised Jesus from the dead, you will be saved. The Holy Spirit will come into your heart and be your guide. You will be set free from your bondage. Will you receive the Lord Jesus into your heart right now?"

Dr. Vic asked the whole congregation to stand. He began to pray, "Heavenly Father, if there's anyone today who is ready to receive you into their heart, man or woman, boy or girl, young or old; if there's someone here who is hurting and wants to be healed; if there's someone who feels like a prisoner and wants to be free, free from sin, free from bondage, free to live a happy life, please let them pray with me: 'Dear Jesus, I confess my sins and I want to be saved. I believe that you died and rose again to save me. I know I'm a sinner. Please forgive me. Please come into my life now. Set me free, and give me a new life. Amen."

When I said that prayer, as soon as I asked for God's forgiveness, the most wonderful thing happened to me. I did not learn about the Holy Spirit until later, but at that moment I felt the Holy Spirit come into my heart like a fluttering butterfly landing on a beautiful flower. Unbelievable joy and overwhelming peace filled my heart. I was suddenly so happy, so light and free of my cares that I felt like I could fly, fly like a butterfly. For the first time in my life, I was free from bondage. It seemed like the whole weight of all the burdens I had ever carried was lifted off me at that moment. I had a new life. I did not know at the time where it would lead me, but without a doubt I had become a new person. I was transformed. Before that moment I had often felt like a worm; now I felt like a butterfly. I was forever changed by God's amazing grace. I knew from that day onward that I was under God's protection. Whatever abuse I might suffer, God would see me through it.

Birds build homes within our boughs,
Our branches shelter grazing cows,
And nature moves around us now
Without communication.

Disowned

MY CONVERSION TOOK PLACE IN AUGUST OF my seventeenth year. I had been living with my cousin Marilee since I lost the baby, and now I was a Christian, a new creature, a new spirit with a new life, and a new beginning. I had hope now that I never had before. I had love in my heart that I never felt—real love. I thanked my cousin Marilee for saving my life, for being there and helping me through all my ordeals. She just smiled and told me again that she loved me and would not let anyone hurt me. "I love you, too, Marilee," I said, "more than you know, and I always will."

My cousin Ginger asked me to come and stay with her for a while. She had three children, two girls and a boy. Her husband, Jack, a tall, thin man, very charming and very nice, was an evangelist who hit the pavement every day telling people about the love of Jesus and the promise of eternal life. He was not paid to do it; he simply wanted people to know the good news of the Gospel.

Jack was once a gang member in Detroit. He had often been in trouble with the law. He was the tenth child in a family of fourteen children. He grew up in poverty and only had a high school education. He got saved, met and married my beautiful cousin, and his whole life turned around. He preached to me the whole time I was there. He read Bible verses to the whole family every day for an hour or so. It was a life I was not familiar with. I had no idea that I was experiencing what many American families do every day. I saw how parents and children loved and respected each other, how a husband should treat his wife, how people can have their own freedom without inhibiting others. Living with Ginger and her family was a true culture shock for me. They were a big influence on me at the beginning of my new life.

My parents did not know anything about my conversion yet. I talked often to my mother on the telephone but did not see her. My mother wanted me to come back home. She repeatedly cried and begged me to come back. She never gave up.

I would refuse and say, "If you can guarantee that I won't get any more beatings and that you'll let me date and have friends, I'll come home."

"Please, Nadia, please come home."

"Can you promise no more beatings?"

"No, Nadia, but I miss you."

"I miss you too, Mama, but I won't allow Baba to beat me again." I remained firm despite the concern I felt for my mother.

So I went from Marilee's to Ginger's for a little over two months. Thanksgiving was near, and I was going to spend it with my cousins. The whole family would get together at Ginger's, since she had a big house. Aunt Grace would be there, too. Thanksgiving was not what I expected. They prayed and thanked God for all the blessings we enjoyed. It was beautiful to me. I had never heard people pray like that. They prayed like they were having a conversation with God. The prayers I was familiar with were repeated over and over again. Their prayers were fresh and meaningful. Their relationship to God was so personal. He was like a good friend to them or part of the family.

God's blessings were plentiful that Thanksgiving, my first as a Christian. Jack asked everyone to say a prayer. I had never prayed aloud before. I kept it simple: "Thank you, God," I said, "but I ate too much."

Everyone laughed. I could hardly stand up. I was stuffed like the turkey. Everyone was stuffed. It was a great day. I called my mother to wish her a Happy Thanksgiving. She cried because I was not home. I told her I had a good Thanksgiving and not to worry about me. I was doing better than ever. I told her about all the love I was receiving, that being free from control and beatings was wonderful, and I never was happier than now.

Still, I did not mention my conversion. I was waiting for the right time. I did not want to get my mother upset over the telephone. I knew my parents would either kill me for it or disown me. Even though they were not strict Muslims, my parents were heavily influenced by the culture of Islam. They would never accept my conversion. I knew there were really only two responses they could make. They would not compromise.

It was not long after Thanksgiving that I decided to return home. I had to see if things would be different. I told my mother I would come home, but if my father touched me for any reason, I would leave and they would never see me again. She agreed. I returned with my Bible packed in my suitcase, along with a few belongings that I had accumulated during my time away from home. My mother was thrilled to see me. My father showed no emotion and said nothing at all. I went over to hug and kiss him, and, as usual, he pulled away from me. Still, I was glad to see him, and I was so happy to see my brothers and sisters. I really missed them. They all looked so much bigger!

The first day at home was pleasant, but after that things did not seem any different than they were before. However, I was different, and my parents noticed it.

"Why are you so happy? What happened to you?" My mother could not contain her curiosity. I knew that she suspected that I had gone to church with my cousins, and she also suspected that I had been dating.

"I'm just enjoying life, Mama," I replied, without giving her details. My mother is persistent and very perceptive. She probed every day.

"Are you having sex?"

"Of course not. I'm just happy, that's all. I date once in a while but nothing more."

My happiness was driving her crazy. She wanted to know every detail of my daily schedule for the past five months. I could see that she still did not trust me. The old feelings of oppression began to flood over me as I listened to my mother's questions. I would have to learn to conquer them. I still had my dreams. I wanted an education. I wanted a career. I wanted to be an actress. I wanted freedom. I vowed to never let opposition rule my spirit again. I was not the same person who had left home several months before. I was a Christian, and I would be strong. I had experienced freedom in Christ, and I was not about to give it up.

I did not expect my parents to applaud my new faith or my freedom. Christians believe that Jesus was and is the Son of God. The Qur'an explicitly says that Allah neither gives birth (denying God the Father) nor is born (denying God the Son). Muslims do believe in the virgin birth of Jesus, but they do not believe that he was the Son of God. They believe that Jesus was only a prophet in a long line of prophets that ended with Mohammed.

I expected the worst from my parents when the time came to tell them of my conversion to Christianity, but I determined to love them no matter what happened. My expectations came true by default one day when I was outside hanging the clothes that I had washed with my mother's washing machine, the same machine with the wringer that I had learned to hate as a child. I was almost finished when I heard my mother scream my name, "*N-a-d-i-a! Yaaaaa, Nadia!*" The formidable side of my diminutive mother surfaced again. I knew I was in deep trouble for something. I ran toward the house, but before I could reach the side door she was already outside beating herself and tearing her clothes.

"What's this?" she demanded. She had my Bible in her hand.

"Are you a Christian now?" She was screaming in my face and waving the Bible wildly.

Before I could answer, my father appeared, grabbed the Bible from her, and threw it into the trash barrel. There were a lot of other papers already there, so, when he lit the trash, the whole barrel was engulfed in flames. He and my mother glared at me for a moment and then went inside the house.

When I went to the barrel, I was astonished! All the trash around my Bible was on fire, but not the Bible. I reached in through the flames and pulled it out. I hid it outside until my parents went to bed. Then I sneaked it back inside and found a much better hiding place for it.

The subject of my conversion was brought up again the next day. Since they had destroyed the Bible, my parents thought that I would not have anything to teach me about Christianity. They believed that I would soon forget about it. They were wrong. I read my rescued Bible late at night and learned to practice the life principles I found there. Ironically, my parents benefited from my Bible reading. For example, the Bible teaches children to respect their parents. It also teaches that the body is the temple of God and that long hair is a woman's glory. My hair was down to my waist. I felt very special about my body being God's temple and my hair my glory.

I also began to look at my parents in a new light. I never cursed them. I never hated them. I cannot say that I always obeyed them. With my new faith, I tried to reconcile with them. I began to obey my parents like I thought God wanted me to, trying to discern when they were right or wrong, of course, but always respecting them because they were my parents.

None of this moved my parents at the time. They were steadfast in their attitude about my conversion, and very soon I would pay dearly for it. I was disowned.

As for the Bible, I still have it. The cover is falling off, and the pages are worn, but there are no burn marks on it. Like me, it was snatched from the fire and destined to survive. It was a gift from Aunt Grace. There is an inscription inside the cover that reads exactly as follows. The grammar falls short of being perfect, but the sentiment is exactly right:

> *To Nadia, a new Christian, a fine young lady I am proud to present this precious Bible to. Praying it will give you spiritual strength to your SALVATION in Christ.   Love, Aunt Grace*

And with the years we older grow,
But no more heights we seem to know,
And every day goes by the same—
A wooden machination.

The Plot

L IFE AT HOME DID NOT GET BETTER. SOMETHING had to be done. I had to find the courage and strength to live on my own. I did not know how I could support myself. I had nowhere to stay. I did not want to burden my cousins again, even though they would have been happy to help me. I was fearful of going too far away from my comfort zone, albeit abusive, but that is all I knew. I had never been completely on my own, even selling magazines. Still, I had to do it. I had dreams to pursue, my own life to live.

One Saturday afternoon, the sun was shining brightly, and I was walking with friends: Teresa, Tommy, Billy, Karen, Donna, and a few others. We were going to the soda shop at the corner of Dix Avenue and Wyoming Street. My father happened to drive by and noticed me in the group. On other occasions he had stopped and dragged me away from my friends. Surprisingly, this time he drove right by. It was not like my father to do that. I could not help but wonder why. I visited with my friends for a while at Cunningham's and went directly home anticipating an ominous confrontation with my father.

I no sooner opened the door to my bedroom upstairs when I heard my father yell, "*Nadia, come down here right now!*" He was not happy.

I calmly went downstairs.

"When are you going to learn?" he growled as he grabbed me and shook me. "When are you going to stay away from the boys and from Teresa?"

"They are my friends, Baba, I wasn't doing anything with them, just talking and walking to Cunningham's to listen to the jukebox. I came home on the condition that you wouldn't beat me anymore. Why are you doing this?" I spoke quietly so as not to provoke him further.

"I'm sick and tired of you," he raged. "You are not going to do whatever you want. I am fed up with you and your ways. You want freedom, you want to be American, and you want boyfriends." He was yelling at me and pushing me backwards. I tripped and fell. He grabbed my arm and began dragging me toward the basement stairs. No one else was home, just the two of us. I screamed for help, but there was no one to hear.

My father proceeded to drag me toward the basement stairs. His fierce grip tightened on my arm.

"What are you going to do to me, Baba?" I screamed. We were at the top of the stairs.

He opened the door and started to drag me down the stairs. "I'm going to hang you and finish with it once and for all. You want to be like the American girls and boys. You don't listen to me. You won't marry one of your cousins. You won't marry an Arab. I'm sick and tired of you, Nadia."

I saw the rope hanging from the basement ceiling pipes. He had planned to kill me when he saw me with my friends. That is why he drove past us. "*No, Baba. No, Baba,*" I cried. "*Don't do this.*"

He gritted his teeth and said, "You're dead to me."

I began to kick and fight, something I had never done before. It had a surprise effect, just as it did with my attacker in Whittier, California. He released his grip just a little, and I fought loose. I ran up the stairs and outside. My father was yelling after me to stop, but I ran faster. I knew he would try to find me, so I ran down the alley, across Wyoming Street, and on and on until I found some bushes to hide in. I hid there for what seemed like a week, until I felt safe enough to come out. My father was nowhere in sight.

I had only enough money for bus fare, so I took the first bus to Michigan Avenue and Schaefer Road, a commercial area. I went store to store trying to think of what to do next. I kept looking over my shoulder for my father. I was afraid to call the police.

Suddenly, a plan came to mind. I decided to steal something and try to get caught. The store manager would call the police, and then I could tell my story. I went into Kresge's dime store and began to look for a target. I saw a key chain with a pink lipstick tube attached to it and put it in my pocket. No one saw me. I looked for another target. I found a small, make-up mirror, took a good, long look at myself in it, and very obviously put it in my pocket.

That did it. A plainclothes security guard confronted me.

"Young lady, what have you got in your pockets?"

"Who, me?" I asked nervously. I was sweating and anxious and thinking that maybe my plan was not so smart after all.

"Yes, you," he said sternly. "Empty your pockets."

I emptied and felt like I was going to pass out. The guard must have called the police after my first snatch, because they were already there by the time I put the marks on the counter. This was the plan, and it was working, but it was working too well! My head was spinning, and I was trembling all over.

The officers took me to the police station, as I hoped they would. I knew I would be safe there. Since my record was clean, they believed my story. A nice woman detective questioned me for a couple of hours about my life and examined my wounds. She was outraged when she saw all the bruises and welts on my body. I gave her details about the attempted hanging.

"How can a parent do this to a child!" she exclaimed sympathetically. I was asked to sign a complaint to put my father in prison. I had déjà vu. History was repeating itself, but it was my father this time rather than Adara and my mother going to prison.

"Are you going to sign?" the detective asked.

"If I do, who will support our family?" I asked.

"There's always welfare, and there are foster homes."

"No, that won't do. I won't sign." I knew that my mother was too proud to go on welfare, and she would be devastated to lose her children.

"All right, it's your decision, but your father is a lucky man. He should be in prison for what he has done to you. Your parents don't deserve you."

"Thank you," I said in a voice that must have sounded very tired.

"You're exhausted," said the detective. "What do you want us to do? Do you have a safe place to stay?"

"I can stay with my cousin," I sighed. I called my cousin Ginger again.

"Of course you can stay here, Nadia, our house is your house," she said.

Knowing that I would not be safe at home alone, the detective asked, "Would you like us to take you home and get your clothes?"

"Yes, please, my parents won't let me leave without a fight," I assured her.

Two police officers drove me home. They got out of the squad car looking very menacing and powerful and knocked on the side door. My father came to the door. I watched from the car as they spoke to my father. I overheard every word that was said.

"Mr. Habibi, Dearborn police. We have your daughter, Nadia, here. She was picked up for shoplifting."

My father's face flushed with anger.

"We're here to get her clothes and take her wherever she wants to go, somewhere far away from you. She used shoplifting as a smart way to call the police. She's a very bright girl. You're lucky she didn't sign a complaint against you, or you'd be under arrest now. Open the door."

My father started to resist the officers. "You have no right to take my daughter," he said angrily.

"Step aside, sir," they said, "or we'll arrest you for obstructing justice."

My father let them pass and began to curse the day I was born. I followed close behind the officers and packed what few things I had. Then the officers helped me into the back seat of the patrol car. As we were pulling out of the driveway, my mother was screaming and crying for me. My father was still shouting curses and threats.

"They will probably come looking for me," I said to the officers.

"If that happens, just call us," they replied.

My cousin Ginger and her family were waiting for me. I told them all about my ordeal at home, the burning of the Bible and being disowned, the continued mistrust, the beatings, and the attempted hanging. Ginger just shook her head. She was speechless for a long time. Then she said tenderly, "How can anyone beat a little thing like you? What do you weigh, ninety pounds? You can stay here as long as you like."

"Thank you, Ginger, I love you," I said, giving her a hug. I meant it with all my heart.

Part Three

Marital Wars

Breakaway

We cast our seeds upon the thrust
Of wind that carries off our trust.
Our children sprout, then grow like us—
Another generation.

Chapel of Love

*T*HE HOLIDAYS SLIPPED BY, AND IT SEEMED SO quiet at times. I missed my family, but not enough to go back and be tormented. I kept myself busy with work, and I was dating Billy occasionally. Whenever he came over, we spent most of our time at Ginger's or Marilee's house playing cards and chatting.

Billy asked to come over one day in early February. He said he had something important on his mind. He looked very serious when he arrived.

"Hi, is Nadia here?"

"Just a second." I heard Marilee's voice from another room, so I went to the door.

Before I could say hello, Billy said nervously, "I need to talk to you. Can we be alone?"

"Of course, let's sit in the living room. No one will bother us there."

"Nadia," he began, "we've known each other for a long time, right?"

"Yes, about four years, I think."

"I've always been there for you, right? I know all about the stuff your parents have put you through and everything else."

"Yes, I guess you do, Billy."

"Nobody knows you like I do, Nadia." He was wiping his sweaty hands on his jeans.

"Are you all right?" I had to ask, because he looked kind of pale.

He went on with his mission: "Nothing that happened to you was your fault, Nadia. I know that. You didn't deserve any of it. You've been very brave. You know I've always loved you, no matter what. I have a question to ask you."

"What, Billy?" I said.

"Nadia, I want to marry you. Will you be my wife?"

I was not expecting this question at all. I was shocked. I was speechless. I just sat there staring at him.

"I'll be good to you, Nadia," he continued. "You can stay with my mother and me until we get married, and then we can get a place of our own. We can . . ."

I had to interrupt. "Billy, I don't know if I'm ready to get married now. I haven't had time to be on my own. I've never had freedom. I need time to think about it. What about my dreams to go to school, to be an actress?"

He was not at all happy with my response. He looked at me glumly and said, "I love you, Nadia. I want to marry you. I thought you loved me, too."

"I do love you," I said gently, "but I need a little time."

"Hell, I didn't expect you to analyze this. I thought you wanted to marry me," he pouted. "If you don't marry me, I'll kill myself." He was already upset at the thought of being rejected.

"No, you won't," I said laughing.

"Yes, I will," he snapped back defensively.

I was actually afraid he might kill himself. I did not want that, but I needed time to think. Is marriage to Billy what I really wanted? I tried to lighten the moment a bit, "Give me a few days to think, Billy, then you can go ahead and kill yourself after that, okay?"

He reluctantly agreed.

I talked to my cousins about Billy's proposal. They thought he was a great guy and that he would take good care of me.

"He loves you, Nadia, see how it works," Marilee said. "You can still go and do all the things you want to. He'll let you, because he knows what you've been through. Billy knows everything about you." Ginger agreed.

"That's true," I said, "I do care about him, too, and I've known him longer than anyone else. I guess I should marry him." The idea of marriage began to appeal to me as I thought it over, although Billy and I were as unprepared for marriage as Adam and Eve. We would be starting out with nothing but each other. I weighed the idea of going on my own into a new life or going into it with the help of someone who loved me. I decided I could use the help. I needed security and safety. I could not impose on my cousins forever, and I could not go home. Billy offered me an alternative. My cousins encouraged me. Billy loved me. I loved him. Why not get married?

Billy came over later that week. I opened the door for him.

"Well, are you goin' to marry me?"

"Yes, Billy, I'll marry you, because I do love you. I guess now you don't have to kill yourself!"

"Guess not," he said with a big smile.

"And you'll never again threaten to kill yourself?"

"Never."

Billy hugged and kissed me and made me feel very confident and secure in my decision. I wanted more than anything to be cherished. I looked forward to building a life together with my childhood sweetheart. For once I was happy. We went together to tell Marilee and Ginger the good news.

We decided to wait until we were both eighteen to get married, so all we would have to do is get a blood test and register for a license. We decided to get married by the Justice of the

Peace. In the intervening months, I decided to simplify things by staying with Marilee. Billy and I could not afford a wedding. We were both flat broke. Imagine getting married with no money and no prospect of a job to make a living. What we had was love. Only love. It has been said that love is blind. It might also be said that it is foolish. We did not even think of the basic necessities. We just wanted to be together.

On a spring day, shortly after my eighteenth birthday, with nothing but young love on our side, we went to the Justice of the Peace. A strange thing happened on the way there. We were walking to the bus stop when I said to Billy, "What if my heel breaks before we get there?"

I do not know why I said it, because there was nothing wrong with my heels. But sure enough, the words were barely out of my mouth when it happened.

"Oh no, Billy, look, my heel did break! What does it mean?"

"Nothing," he responded quickly.

"Maybe it's a sign," I continued. "Maybe it means we shouldn't get married right now. What if it's a sign that something isn't right? What if it means bad luck is coming to us? What if it means we'll break up?"

"Are you crazy?" he shot back. "You're just being superstitious. Let's go." He was getting upset, so I put it out of my mind.

When the bus arrived, Billy took my arm and helped me board. In no time, we were downtown at the office of the Justice of the Peace. I had to get married with one shoe on and one off! I was quite embarrassed, but there was no turning back.

We stood like statues in front of the Justice of the Peace. He seemed so intimidating in his black robe. I was an introvert, and Billy was just as bad as I was. We were terrified. I began to tremble. "Am I doing the right thing?" I asked myself. "On the other hand, if I don't go through with this, Billy will kill himself. I have to do this." At the time, I was not aware of a rule that I have followed many times later in life: that doubts are don'ts. I kept my thoughts to myself, and, while I was thinking, the Justice of the Peace said, "I now pronounce you man and wife."

That was it. No frills. No fuss. No muss.

The honeymoon was the shortest ever. We had none. Billy kissed me. The judge shook Billy's hand and wished us luck. He came over to me and gave me a hug. We said our thanks, and that was that. I was married to Billy, for better or worse. It might have been for richer, but it could not have been for poorer, because we had nothing. As for sickness and health—well, read on.

I did not tell my parents about marrying Billy. I knew they would be against it, so I said nothing. Billy and I stayed with his mother for a couple of months before Billy found a job and an apartment. Billy's mother was old and very ill with diabetes. She was stout (not to say obese) and very tired after birthing and raising ten children. Billy was her baby. I never saw them together for more than two minutes before our marriage, but now I saw a different side of Billy and his mother. They loved each other completely.

Billy would do anything for his mother, and she knew it. She had to give herself injections and drink a glass of orange juice every day to manage the diabetes. He helped with that. She chewed tobacco, too. I had never known a woman to chew tobacco or give herself a shot. She claimed that most people in Tennessee chew tobacco. I thanked God that Billy did not chew. I could not stand the dirty coffee cans half-filled with sawdust and tobacco juice always stationed around the house. I resigned myself to the fact that it was her house and vowed that it would never happen in mine!

While Billy did not share his mother's appetite for tobacco, they liked to drink beer together. Billy was sent out to buy a couple six-packs every day. They would each drink one. I had no experience with beer drinking. Muslims are teetotalers, so there was never any beer in the house when I grew up. None of the Arabs I knew drank. Billy said he needed it to cool off on hot summer days. His mother did not need a reason to drink. Hot or cold, she just drank. Every day.

Billy went job hunting and finally found one as a chef's helper at one of the most exclusive restaurants in town. He was well liked. I would often go there to walk home with him after work. He introduced me to all the kitchen help.

"This is my wife, Nadia," he liked to say to them. It sounded weird to be referred to as his wife, but it was nice, and it was good for Billy to feel so proud.

"This is your pretty, little wife? You look good together, Billy." They all gushed over him. "You take good care of her or you'll hear from us." The women all told me how wonderful he was and how handsome and what beautiful blue eyes he had.

I thanked them and agreed, "yes, he certainly is," and "yes, he surely has." They said he was doing a great job. He was smiling from ear to ear, shyly accepting the adulation. I did not see them often, since we were moving into our own apartment, and I had a lot of work to do, but they seemed like a very decent crowd.

To say that we had but few possessions is putting it mildly. I spent most of my time cleaning and cooking, getting things ready for Billy to come home from work. I wanted our place to be nice for him. The apartment was an upstairs flat, and, fortunately, it was furnished. The landlord was an elderly man who lived with his son on the first floor. His son was shell-shocked during World War II. He needed constant care. I remember him sitting at the table all day rapidly drumming his fingers. It was scary to me. I had never known anyone who was shell-shocked. I felt sorry for him. While Billy was at work, I frequently went downstairs to visit the two men. I had no car, so I spent a lot of my spare time with them. They appreciated the company.

Very soon after we were married, I was hired at the Acme Precision factory in Detroit. Acme manufactured automobile parts. I worked there for a month and was promoted to line supervisor by the foreman. This move made all the other female workers as mad as hell. They thought that I was given the job because I was sleeping with the foreman. I was not. He wanted it that way, but I was faithful to Billy. I quit after three months. I had enough of the jealousy and rumors. The pay was not worth it.

Breakaway

Without my check, money was short, and we began to have marital problems. Billy began to stay longer at work. When he did come home late, he always had a supply of beer with him. I would have dinner waiting for him, but it always had to be warmed up. After dinner, he parked himself in front of the TV and drank his beer.

We began to fight. I wanted some quality time with my husband. He wanted to drink and have his own space. Now that he was working, he felt he deserved his beer and time alone. The more he drank, the more he wanted. When he was so drunk he could hardly stand up, he wanted to have sex.

It did not take long before I became disgusted with this routine. I especially hated the idea of having sex with a drunken husband, but if I did not respond, he would force himself on me. I learned that there are two kinds of rape: one outside of marriage and one in it.

What had I got myself into? Our lives had become a rut. Billy came home late, drank, wanted sex, and went to sleep. I voiced my frustration more frequently as the weeks turned to months. "Billy, I'm fed up with this. You come home late. You're drinking all the time. All you do is sit and watch TV with a beer in your hand. You're like a robot. I'm trying to make a home for us, and where are you? I cook and clean and wait for you to come home so we can have time together, but you don't care. It's like we're not even married."

It was useless. I was talking to the air. He did not listen to a word I said. He continued with the routine, and things got worse. They always do if they do not get better.

One day, Billy was late from work again. One hour, two hours, three hours went by very slowly, and still there was no Billy. Where was he? My mind was in turmoil. Did he have an accident? Was he in the hospital? I was getting frantic. I called the police to see if they had a report about him. They did not. I called his mother. She had not heard from him. I was getting hysterical. It was seven thirty, and still I had not heard from my husband. The apartment was clean. The dinner was cold. All I had to do was worry. I even thought he might be dead.

Around eight o'clock, I heard some scuffling on the stairs. Someone was dragging something up to our apartment. I opened the door, and there was Billy. He was dead drunk. He could barely hurl himself forward, and he looked like a crushed vehicle. He was struggling to stand up. I grabbed him under the arms to help support his weight and pointed him toward the bed. It was like walking a dead body. He reeked of booze and vomit. The smell permeated the room and hung in the air, stale and putrid. The forced journey over, he fell into bed and immediately passed out. In bed with him was not where I would be this night. I decided to sleep on the sofa, but first I trashed his dinner.

I left him alone for fear he would get mad and become violent with me as he did more and more frequently. Although my father was never under the influence of alcohol, the beatings Billy delivered were much like his. A typical evening went like this: empowered to machismo by alcohol, Billy attacked me with his fists, always without the least provocation, until I was knocked down, whereupon he saved himself the effort of bending over by kicking me around the apartment. The abuse lasted until his strength waned. I put up with it. I was a veteran. I had taken all the best punches and kicks my father could deliver. Men are beaters— all of them. It is what they do. That is what I thought.

The next morning, life went on as if nothing had happened. Billy went to work, and he stayed late. He spent some of his wages and brought home just enough to pay the rent and buy groceries. He lived for beer and sex. If he did not get both, he became violent. I never bought beer for him, but I could not refuse him sex. He repeatedly said he only wanted to drink and have sex. Responsibilities he did not want.

I wondered what happened to the old Billy, the listener, the sympathetic caregiver, the lover, and the friend. I wondered why courtship was so different from marriage. Which Billy was the real person? I should have guessed that marriage for Billy was all about satisfying his own needs. That is why he threatened to kill himself.

He was all right if he got what he wanted, but he was not thinking of me. It was all about him.

I decided the real Billy was a mix of both good and bad qualities. The problem was that alcohol opened the door for the abuser to come out. Billy could still be sweet without the booze, but less and less so as time went on. I began to see that he was very insecure. The insecurity ultimately led him to become insanely jealous of me.

One night, Billy came home drunk as usual. Through his slurred speech I came to understand that he had been to a bar. There he met a woman who also was drunk. He said they talked and slow danced, but that was all. Nothing more. "Thanks for telling me, Billy, I really appreciate that," I said coldly.

I did not know about the guilt-blame teeter-totter at the time. If I had, I might have been able to understand Billy's behavior better. I know now that when people are guilty of something, they often blame others for things they are doing themselves, when, in fact, the others are completely innocent. The accuser feels less guilty by trying to bring the other person down to his level. It helps him to balance his unacceptable behavior with the unattainable standards of society. He cannot bring himself up, so he pulls others down.

Billy's extracurricular activities at the bar and elsewhere led him to accuse me of all kinds of things I did not do. One evening, I left him at the apartment while I went to pick up the Chinese food we had ordered. The restaurant was only a few blocks away. Billy followed me, concealing himself in doorways and behind trees like a detective in a B-rated movie. Unfortunately, a car filled with hormone-driven boys came down our street. The boys all but fell out the windows whistling and honking at me. The stalking Billy observed this, made a string of inaccurate calculations in his jealous mind, came out of hiding, and accosted me. He blamed me for soliciting the boys and sent me home. He would get the Chinese food himself.

Two hours passed and Billy was not home yet. If I had eaten Chinese food, I would have been hungry again by then. Two more hours passed, and Billy finally appeared. He was intoxicated, of course, in the usual rage, and, predictably, without the Chinese food.

"You whhhhore," he bellowed, having trouble directing his speech from his alcohol-soaked brain. "I ssssssaw you fffflirtin' with those boys. Guys only dooooo that if girlssssss lead them on."

"Oh, yeah, that's right, Billy. I can't help it if guys honk and whistle at me. I was just walking on the sidewalk, as you could see for yourself. How else could I go to the Chinese restaurant and back?" I spoke calmly and deliberately, but to no avail since he was intent on his mission.

"Issss your fault when guys llllook at you annnn 'onnnk their 'orns. Annn you like it, dooonnn you? You're shhheating on me, ain't you?" His own words were fueling his jealousy.

"No, Billy," I replied coldly, "I'm not cheating on you. I swear I'm not."

"Liar. I dooonnn believe you," he ranted. Then, just like my father, Billy grabbed my long hair, my glory and crown, and, despite his drunken state, threw me to the floor, stomping and kicking me like a bag of corn until I could not get up. I cried and cried for him to stop, but he would not until he had exhausted himself.

I thought that I had married Billy. In reality, I married my father. There was no real significant difference between their behaviors. The same rogues lived in both of their houses, the main ones being control, distrust, and jealousy. I do not mean to take away their individual responsibility for their cruel acts. Not at all, but something triggered the violent, raging person that they both became under certain circumstances. Alcohol was the catalyst for Billy. Male dominance and cultural traditions influenced my father. I do not believe that either of them understood what the trigger was, but they were as dangerous as an automatic weapon in the hands of a fanatic when the trigger was pulled. There was no stopping them until they completely fired whatever ammunition they had. Until I found the strength to break away, I was simply the target of their wrath.

Breakaway

Billy never believed me. The pattern of his insane jealousy, philandering, drinking, and beatings became predictable and all too frequent. Why, I kept asking myself, was abuse always happening to me? I had hoped that things would be different with Billy. I believed that I had left home for happiness. The truth is that I only left Hell for Hades.

What was I to do?

What will they be? What will they do?
Our worried bark is furrowed through.
All our hopes and dreams are wrapped
In pure exasperation.

Having My Baby

THE CHILL OF WINTER WAS ALREADY IN THE AIR by early November. A few stubborn leaves remained on the maples and oaks where vivid reds, oranges, and yellows had dressed October. Soon snow-laden clouds driven by icy blasts of Arctic air would unburden themselves and launch us into six months of my least favorite season. I hated cold weather. I found no redeeming factors in it. I remembered the blue Pacific and the swaying palms of sunny California and imagined that one day I would live there, probably in Hollywood as a famous actress.

The approach of winter found Billy and me living in an upstairs flat on Canterbury Street in Dearborn. A single mom with three children lived downstairs. They existed on welfare. I had never known anyone on welfare before. She explained to me that without help from the state, she would not be able to feed her children. I wondered what she did all day, since she did not work. Her house was filthy, and she did not take good care of her children. Most of the time they wore soiled clothes that looked like they had not been washed for weeks. I felt sorry for them, and I tried to help whenever I could. My efforts ceased one day when I felt sick to my stomach. I knew the feeling. I was pregnant.

Despite the problems that Billy and I had not worked through, I determined to look on the bright side. I was married this time. I was not raped. There would be no illegal abortion. I was sincerely happy to be pregnant.

I set up an appointment with Dr. Chase, the same doctor who saved my life by removing the garden hose. He remembered me and was so happy to see me again.

"You're married, and now you're pregnant," he said, putting his arm around me.

"Yes, and if it weren't for you, I wouldn't be either of those. I wouldn't be here at all," I smiled and thanked him again. I asked him a lot of questions about pregnancy. I still did not know how a child was conceived. I did not know about the uterus and the sperm and the egg. I really did not know what to expect during the pregnancy either. He was amazed at my innocence and naiveté, and he happily answered all of my questions.

"Don't ever be afraid to ask questions," he said. "I understand how you were kept in a bottle when you were at home. It's not uncommon. I treat a surprising number of ladies with your background who have no idea about how their bodies work. Sex is something that is done to them, not something they understand. Lack of education is a big problem in our community. Anyway, you're already about a month into your pregnancy, so you can expect to have a baby about the middle of June."

"Great, before it gets too hot," I responded. "I'll be able to enjoy the rest of the summer without a big stomach."

He laughed and took several pamphlets off the counter in the exam room and handed them to me.

"Read these, Nadia. They will help you understand what's happening to you and how you can best manage your pregnancy. I'm so happy to see you're doing well. Please contact me right away if you have a problem or a question. My staff will call you when it's time for your next visit."

"Thank you, Dr. Chase, thank you very much." I was so grateful for this man. I didn't tell him about all the difficulties I was having with Billy. I didn't want to spoil the moment.

Billy came home from work and before he sat down with his beer I said, "Guess what? Guess what?" I was glowing with excitement.

"What?" he asked.

"I'm pregnant! I'm going to have our baby!" I exclaimed. "Dr. Chase says I'm about a month along."

Billy smiled and hugged me, "Great," he said, "Great, I'm goin' to be a daddy."

"Yeah, and I'm going to be a mom," I replied, "and I want this baby to have all our love and whatever else it needs. I never want him or her to lack for anything."

"Everything will be okay," Billy assured me. "When's the baby goin' to be born?"

"June!" I shouted over my shoulder on my way to the kitchen. No, I was not barefoot there! I was, however, ecstatic that my life seemed to be turning in a new direction. I would do everything in my power to give my child the kind of life I never had.

Breakaway

We learn we can't do otherwise,
The years have somehow made us wise.
We cannot live our lives through them—
A brilliant observation.

Roaches

HE MONTHS OF THE PREGNANCY PASSED, AND
my baby was born. During the thirty-six hours of labor, I
swore up and down that I would never get pregnant
again! I could not imagine going through an encore of all that pain,
but I immediately forgot the oaths when I saw my baby boy for the
first time! He was beautiful! He was so small, so very tiny. I held
him close to my heart and cried with joy. "My baby belongs to me
and no one else; he's totally mine," I thought to myself.

I became completely immersed in taking care of my baby. I
forgot about everything else. I did not pray or go to church, and, of
course, I did not see my family anymore. I became a recluse,
giving all my time to the baby and to Billy. Throughout the
pregnancy, Billy was drinking almost every night and coming
home at late hours. He was out bar hopping, dancing, and having
affairs with other women. Most of the time we fought. Of course,
he accused me of cheating on him. None of that mattered now. My
happiness was complete in my baby. I named him Hunter.

The birth of Hunter gave me new life and hope. He needed me and I needed him. He was *my* baby. During the pregnancy, I did not eat very well or often enough. Billy could not keep a regular job, so there were times when we were short on groceries. When he did work, he often brought home a pink slip instead of money. His drinking got him fired.

I became anemic so that when Hunter was born, he was anemic as well. I spent one month in the hospital with him, feeding him and loving him to health. He was five pounds and five ounces at birth and nineteen inches long. He was a beautiful baby with thick, black hair that was long and silky smooth. His eyes were dark brown, and his skin was milky white with a hint of olive. I loved him completely, and I was the happiest I had ever been.

I was also tired most of the time. I took care of Hunter and his feedings all by myself. I was sleep deprived. Once, while making the formula for Hunter, I fell asleep in the kitchen chair and forgot the milk bottles on the stove. The smoke-filled kitchen and the odor of burnt milk finally woke me up. I ran to the stove and turned off the burner. The bottles were cracked and ruined, and the formula, of course, was wasted which meant that my baby had none. I opened all the windows and hurried to the bedroom to remove Hunter from the apartment until the smoke cleared. I was devastated to think how much worse it might have been. I thanked God that I fell asleep in the kitchen, close to the stove.

Billy came home and yelled at me for being so negligent. I told him that if he had helped me with taking care of Hunter once in a while, it would not have happened. I did not need a lecture on how to take care of babies. I needed sleep. I was familiar with babies and feedings. For much of my childhood I took care of my mother's babies. I often got up in the middle of the night to feed my siblings so she could get a good night's rest. My father did not help her either. Apparently, the care and feeding of babies was not something that males did. It was always my job. Sometimes experiences are bittersweet, usually bitter at the time but sweeter in hindsight. My motherly duties robbed me of my childhood, but they prepared me to care for my own children.

Breakaway

One night, I got up to get the baby his bottle and to find a snack for myself. Billy, as usual, was sound asleep. Several giant, ugly roaches greeted me when I opened the cupboard. Roaches I cannot endure. I screamed and woke Billy up. He was not happy. He was even less so when I grabbed him by the hair and screamed, *"Get me out of here!"* He got the point. I could not cope with the idea of roaches crawling on my baby.

I was so scared from that time forward, I had a tough time falling asleep, no matter how deprived. I kept watch over Hunter for hours, making sure no roaches were crawling into his crib. The last straw for me was when I went downstairs to the neighbor lady's apartment and accidentally knocked a wicker clothesbasket off the shelf. Hundreds of roaches came rushing down from the sides of the basket like a black waterfall. I realized at that moment why I had roaches upstairs. My screams echoed throughout the building. I set my mind to get my baby out of that building as soon as possible. I did not want to wait another minute. Billy came home that evening to find me packing. He was sober for a change.

"What's goin' on?" he demanded.

"I'm leaving," I said vehemently. He looked like I hit him with a rock.

"I'm so sorry," he said, "I'll try harder. You deserve a better husband."

"For once, it's not you," I said. "I want us out of this roach-invested hole today. The whole place is overrun with roaches."

I related the ordeal with the roaches downstairs in the neighbor's basket. He agreed that we should move as soon as I could find another apartment. I wasted no time. I found an apartment in Detroit, and we moved that very week.

The apartment was poorly furnished, but it was clean. It was located near Coplin Street and Jefferson Avenue, not far from Grosse Pointe, the richest community in the Detroit area. Only wealthy executives, doctors, and lawyers lived there. No blacks were allowed, and poor people like us could not afford to even have a salad at one of their exclusive restaurants. I did not need to live in Grosse Pointe, but I insisted on having a clean place free of roaches.

Once we had established ourselves in Detroit, Billy's mother and sisters moved there, too. Billy had eight sisters and one brother. I had met the sisters but not the brother. He was serving a long prison term. I was surprised that no one ever talked about him. Most of Billy's sisters were alcoholics like him. They went to bars in the evening while their husbands were at work. They left young children sleeping alone at home while they got drunk and trolled for men. I wanted to call the children's welfare department and report them, but Billy would not let me.

One of the sisters was named Selma. She was a tall, lanky brunette whose conduct was deplorable. She would go out all night, leaving her babies alone, hungry, and swimming in soaked diapers. After a night of prowling, Selma would drag home a drunk and perform sex acts with him in front of her children or anyone else unfortunate enough to be present. I was sick about it and could not tolerate it anymore. I called the children's welfare department and anonymously reported her. Needless to say, I had nothing to do with that sister.

The cockroach is an inveterate pest. Once it gets established, the roach is very hard to get rid of. Billy's sister, Beulah, was a pest not unlike the cockroach. She had a long list of bad habits, and she was virtually impossible to remove from the premises. She was a heavy drinker, and she was sexually promiscuous above all the rest. Worst of all, she had incestuous desires for Billy, and she lived under the illusion that our apartment was hers. No cockroach was less welcome.

Beulah interfered with our marriage in ways that cannot be described. She was extremely jealous of me. She wanted Billy and his bed for herself. She came over almost every day and would take Billy out with her to the bars. It might be days before he returned home. When he did, he immediately began to beat me to relieve his guilt. I left him several times because of Beulah, but he always found me and coaxed me to come home. He promised not to go with Beulah and get drunk, promised to be a better husband and father, promised, promised, and promised.

It never happened.

Breakaway

So back the question comes again,
Like music of an endless strain—
What is the purpose of a tree?
Our self-interrogation.

Crazy Leon

AFTER SEVERAL MORE MONTHS OF HELL WITH Billy and his family, we got the news that his brother Leon was out of prison. No one knew his whereabouts, but they hoped he would contact one of them. He made contact all right. Somehow he had heard about Billy and me and our baby Hunter. He found out where we lived and made a surprise visit.

Billy was at work at one of the factories in Detroit. We had been forced to move again, because Billy could not pay the weekly rent. Now we lived on Fairview Street. We had rented an upstairs apartment. Billy had the swing shift, so he was gone most nights. Hunter was still an infant in the crib. I fed him and tucked him in; he looked so peaceful and so happy that night. I fell asleep, too, always tired from sleep deprivation. Perhaps I was an over-protective mother. Be that as it may, I had heard too many stories about crib deaths, so I watched over him during the night hours to make sure he was breathing.

I was deeply asleep around midnight. I thought I was dreaming when I felt a knife at my throat. A man was holding me down and whispering, "Don't scream or I'll kill you."

"Who are you?" I managed to ask.

"Leon," he said.

"Leon who?" My voice came out so calmly that I surprised myself.

"Leon, your brother-in-law."

"How did you get in here?"

"It's my secret," he whispered.

"Are you going to kill me?" I wondered aloud. I was, under the circumstances, not the least bit nervous. I was thinking about my baby and the need to protect him.

"Just do as I say and nobody gets hurt. You sure are beautiful."

"Is it okay if I sit up?"

"Sure, but don't do anything stupid." He let me up but kept me at knifepoint.

"Do you mind if I check on my baby?"

"Go ahead. Don't worry, darlin', I didn't do anything to your baby. I didn't come here for the baby. I'm waitin' here till Billy gits home, and then you and I is leavin' together."

"*What!*" I shouted. I might have asked him if he was crazy, but that was already too apparent. I got up warily and checked on Hunter while Leon followed with the knife.

"You're goin' with me," he repeated firmly. "I love you, darlin'."

"Leon, you don't love me. I don't know you, and you don't know me. You're not making sense. How can you love me? Besides, I'm married to your brother." I was buying time. Hunter was still asleep.

"If Billy loves you, I love you, too. I'm goin' to tell Billy you let me in. I'll tell him we had sex. He'll believe me. He won't want you anymore, and you'll have to go with me." Leon indicated that he wanted me to sit on the sofa, while he pulled up a chair a few feet away.

"You're crazy!" The words came freely and automatically. I could not resist. It was trite to say it, but no truth was ever more clearly stated. "Billy would never believe such an idiotic thing!"

"Okay, just wait and see," insisted the crazy man. "If he don't believe me, then I gotta kill him." He pointed at the knife and made a jabbing motion with it.

The mention of Billy's potential murder stunned me. I tried to think of ways to carry on the conversation but could not. The silence was heavy, and I worried about the knife in Leon's hand. I had just checked on Hunter, so I could not ask to do that again. Leon just sat there staring at me. His eyes were glazed over and they seemed to radiate a weird, green color in the dim light of the living room.

I tried to remain calm, but a train of questions tracked through my mind. The voice inside my head seemed to come from someone else, some perverse alien siding with crazy Leon. "As crazy as this guy is, he's nothing if not Billy's brother," it said. "Why wouldn't Billy believe him before he believes you? Billy never trusted you anyway. If he thinks you cheat while he's at work, and he cheats with his sisters, why wouldn't he believe that you cheated with his brother? Billy's own record on telling the truth isn't very good, why should he recognize the truth?"

The longer we sat in silence, the more likely it seemed to me that I might be called a liar. In any event, I knew there would be trouble. Billy was due to come home any minute. There was nothing I could do but wait. Every time I moved, Leon waved the knife at me. It did not take a genius to figure out that he was crazy enough to use it.

I finally decided to talk about something familiar to Leon, hoping to ease the tension. I asked him about why he went to prison. What was it like there? Why wasn't he closer to his family? He did not seem to mind talking about prison. He answered all my questions, but he got a little agitated when I asked him about the family. He said he was the firstborn child. He was always the black sheep. He never got along with his sisters, and he did not really know Billy at all, since he was the baby. He was jealous of the attention that Billy got, and he hated the fact that Billy was so good-looking and popular with women. "Billy was always the pet," he complained. "He always got whatever he wanted. I got nothin'."

I started to explain that I, too, was the eldest in my family and got nothing, but decided against it, as I did not want to compare myself to a lunatic. Suddenly, there was a click at the door. Billy turned the key. I saw the knob move, and just as he began to open the door, Leon jumped up and stood behind it with the knife raised and ready.

"*Look out, Billy!*" I screamed. Billy pushed the door open, and Leon jumped out from behind it, pointing the knife at his brother's throat.

"*Hey, what the hell!*" Billy shouted.

"I came by to visit you, Billy boy," Leon said casually, keeping the knife at Billy's throat. "But you was at work, so we's been havin' a nice little time together, if you know what I mean." He dropped his eyes toward his crotch, leaving no doubt in Billy's mind what he meant. "She says you'd be happy to see me. I got outta the tank yesterday. I missed you, little brother. Your wife sure is beautiful. She's comin' with me. She's leavin' you, Billy, an' goin' with me."

I gasped in disbelief. Billy's expression showed that he was buying every word. He seemed to be mesmerized.

"*Billy, he's lying! I didn't tell him that. Don't believe him!*"

Leon motioned toward me with his free hand. "You let me in, darlin', how else did I git in here?"

"*I don't know,*" I screamed, "*but I didn't let you in.*"

"Well," Billy said, "if she wants to go with you, then I guess I'll have to let her go."

"*What! You're both out of your minds!*"

Whether Leon relaxed because he believed Billy or was distracted by my yelling, luckily he dropped his guard, and Billy attacked. They struggled for the knife. Billy grabbed Leon by the arm and slammed it into the door. The knife fell to the floor. I picked it up and ran to the kitchen. They were really going at it, fists flying, both landing blow after blow. Leon quickly had a cut over his eye. Both men had bloody noses. They were yelling at each other and pounding away. In no time, their eyes were black and blue and their mouths looked like Portobello mushrooms. There was blood everywhere.

Someone in the building called the police station (emergency 911 had not been implemented yet). By the time the police got there, the fight was pretty much over, since both men were exhausted. The officers easily broke it up and handcuffed Leon. They asked me a lot of questions, and I gave them a detailed rundown of what happened.

"Do you want to press charges?" They explained that Leon would immediately go back to prison if we did. "He'll be written up for breaking and entering as well as assault with a deadly weapon. He'll be put away for a long time."

"Absolutely," I said without blinking, "take him away."

Billy seemed hesitant about my decision. Leon had just got out of prison, and his mother would not be thrilled about his going back, especially under the circumstances. She would blame Billy and me for sending him to prison.

I did not care. I signed the papers to press charges, and the officers took Leon away. Billy and I stayed up most of the night fighting about what really happened. Billy actually believed his loony brother. I repeatedly told him that I did not let Leon in, but all my words fell on deaf ears. I told him the story from beginning to end, and still he thought I wanted to be with Leon.

"Think about it, Billy, if I really wanted to be with Leon, why would I press charges and put him back in prison? Are you crazy, too? Your whole family is nuts." I was angry and hurt.

Billy came at me like a raging bull and punched me in the face. "Don't you dare call me crazy, you bitch! I knew I couldn't trust you. Go with Leon, I don't care."

I argued vehemently, but still I could not convince Billy that I was innocent. "Let's not keep going over this, Billy, I'm tired. You're not going to believe me anyway. I've never done anything with another man. There's no reason not to trust me. We have a beautiful baby boy, and you should be happy. You're the one who cheats on me and goes out drinking and carousing all the time."

I turned and walked away. The punch in the face was painful, but not as bad as the stab in my heart. I was worried about my baby and his future. What was going to happen to us? I fell asleep thinking of the nightmare that I had just gone through. How was I going to get out of this mess?

A silent voice within reveals
It is not ours to break the seals.
By faith believe what God conceals—
A noble revelation.

Let Me In

THE PHONE RANG EARLY IN THE MORNING, jangling me out of a deep sleep. I forced myself to answer it. Billy's mother was on the line yelling and cursing me for putting Leon back in prison. She did not care about the details, especially from me. I was not from Tennessee, I did not drink, I did not chew, and she did not like me very much, so whatever Leon did to me did not matter to her. She was jealous of my relationship with Billy. She felt that I took him away from her. She forgot that she had abandoned him when he was a child. Her doting on him was probably a compensation for her own guilt.

I pushed and pulled Billy to wake him up so he could handle his mother. It took a while, but finally I succeeded. Billy could sleep through a tornado.

"Here, talk to your mother. She's upset at both of us."

Billy tried to calm her down. Leon was right about one thing. She favored Billy because he was her baby. She listened to him, but she was not to be dissuaded. Billy was holding the phone a foot away from his ear, and I could hear her yelling.

"Git your brother outta jail today," she demanded. "He made a mistake, but he ain't hurt nobody. Git him out! *Git him out now!*"

"Okay, okay, Ma, I will. But he better leave Nadia and me alone and never bother us again, or I'll kill him." Billy was shouting too and sounded convincing.

His mother went ballistic. She turned up the volume: "*Don't you talk like that there 'bout your big brother. You ain't gonna kill nobody. Don't you talk like that there! You wanna go to jail, too?*"

"No," Billy yelled back. "No, I don't want to go to jail, but he has no business bothering us. *You tell him to stay away or else.*"

Billy responded like that for good reason. While I was asleep, he got up and went to the kitchen. He noticed that the window was not completely closed, and the screen was missing. He opened the back door to the apartment and went out to the porch. There he found the screen leaning against the building. That was how his brother got into the apartment. Leon removed the screen, lifted the window, and crawled in. I did not hear him, because I was tired and in a deep sleep.

"So that's how Leon got into the apartment!" I exclaimed. "See, I told you I didn't do it. Now do you believe me?"

"Yes, Nadia, I believe you now. I was wrong. I'm sorry." I believe he really meant it.

Leon was released from custody after a few days, but we never heard from him again. Things returned to normal for a while, at least normal for us. Billy was drinking as usual, coming home angry at something, and blaming me for it. It seemed he always found a reason to beat me. When he was drunk, he was an ogre. Sober, he was a loving lamb. I always thought he would change, stop drinking, and stop the beatings. But he did not change. A leopard does not change its spots.

When Billy was sober, we sometimes took pleasant walks to a park about a mile away from the apartment. Hunter was already thirteen months old and weighed about twenty-two pounds. He was a big boy. Hunter was learning to walk by standing and holding on to things for stability, and he was able to say mama and dada. He hugged me and kissed my face whenever I carried him. I loved it when he sucked my cheeks. I would laugh aloud when he did it, and he would giggle.

I was pregnant again, about two months along. I was happy about it, because my babies would be only nineteen months apart. My hope was that because they were close in age they would grow up to be more than just siblings. I wanted them to be close friends as well. I knew it would be hard for me to manage two babies, but I would do my best for them. I also knew I was going to have a boy again. We did not have ultrasound in those days, but I knew intuitively that this baby would be a boy, just as I had known during my pregnancy with Hunter. I had no doubt about it.

One sunny afternoon in July, Billy and I decided to go to the park, as we often did. We packed a couple of sandwiches, and Billy insisted on taking a six-pack of beer. I was not too happy about it, but I was tired of arguing with him all the time. The sun was filtering through the groves of maples and elms in the park. We sat beneath an elm tree for shade. It was so relaxing. Hunter was happy and talking in baby gibber. He loved the outdoors, as I did. I loved the warmth of the sunshine on my face, but I preferred shade now. I did not want to stay long in the sun. I believed my cultural tradition that if a pregnant woman sits in the sun too long, her baby will be born with burns all over its face and body. I did not think of myself as superstitious, but the idea did bother me a little, and I was not going to risk it.

Billy was guzzling his beer. He said it cooled him off. Before I knew it, he had drunk the whole six-pack in less than an hour. I looked at him, and he was already intoxicated.

"Billy, why did you drink so fast and so much at one time?"

The beer caused him to lose his inhibitions, as it always did. He began to feel amorous, so he grabbed me and wanted to kiss me. He was swaying back and forth like a palm tree in a hurricane.

"Let's have sex right here. C'mon, baby, give me some lovin'." The palm leaned far to the right and almost uprooted itself.

"Are you crazy, Billy?" I was afraid he would become aggressive. "I'm going home. You do what you want."

"You're not leavin'. You're stayin' here. I'm gonna get some love right here." He was insistent, and I could see his temperature rising.

"Oh no, you're not, Billy!" I put Hunter on my left hip. He was heavy and not easy for me to carry.

"*Stop it, Billy! Stop it! Leave me alone!*" He was trying to rape me in the park. No one saw us, or, if they did, no one came to help.

I screamed again, "*Stop it, Billy! Leave me alone!*"

He did not listen and started tearing off my clothes. I began to run away from him. He attempted to run after me, but he was really swaggering and not making much forward progress. I decided to put it into high gear and leave him behind. I ran the entire mile to the apartment without stopping. Hunter was riding sidesaddle, and I was sobbing the whole way. "Please, God, help me," I kept saying it over and over to myself. I ran as fast as I could, not looking back once. I reached the apartment, took the stairs two steps at a time, hurriedly opened the door for Hunter and me, and locked it behind us.

About fifteen minutes or so later, Billy came knocking and yelling, "*Let me in, Nadia! Open the door, or I'll knock it down.*"

Billy finished the sentence and promptly kicked the door open. Hunter was crying. I was crying. Billy rushed in with fire in his belly. He came after me, grabbed my hair and threw me down on the floor, kicking and punching me.

"Billy, please don't do this, please, you'll hurt the baby!" He did not care. I was worried about my baby, not the pain. I did not want to miscarry. I was also trying desperately to get to Hunter, to pick him up and comfort him. He was frightened and crying loudly. Billy paused to catch his breath, and I crawled over to Hunter.

"It's okay, it's okay, I love you, baby," I assured him, holding him tightly. He whimpered and stopped crying.

Billy came after me again as I was picking myself up from the floor. He kicked me really hard on the left calf. It was a violent kick with his steel-toed shoe. I had been hurt before with his beatings, but I knew this was different. The pain was excruciating, and it did not stop. I knew he would keep on beating me if I cried, so I clenched my teeth and kept silent, lying still on the floor. Until now, Billy had done nothing to harm Hunter, but I did not trust him. I lay there for some time until the thought suddenly came to me that I would kill Billy if he hurt my baby.

"You can beat me all you want," I vowed aloud, "but if you touch my baby, I will kill you, Billy." I meant it with all my heart, but my words fell on deaf ears. The fury was gone from Billy. He was fast asleep on the bed.

Breakaway

There is a point where compromise
Will not put up with further lies.
It's then we find within our hearts
A quiet consolation.

Bang! Bang!

*A*T 3:34 ON THE MORNING OF JULY 23, 1967, AN undercover cop bought a beer at a blind pig on Twelfth Street and Clairmount in Detroit. A blind pig, sometimes called a booze can or blind tiger, is a place of business that sells alcoholic beverages illegally. The name derives from the practice of saloonkeepers in the 1800s. Laws governing moral behavior (known as blue laws) forbid the sale of beer or liquor on certain days, usually Sunday, or after certain hours. The speakeasy managers found a way around the law by charging a cover fee for customers to see an attraction, like a blind pig, then serving complimentary beverages. The blind pig law in Detroit was in effect after 2:00 a.m.

Within minutes of the sting, eighty-two arrests were made by the Detroit vice squad, and the ensuing confrontation with patrons started one of the worst riots in United States history, surpassed only by the Los Angeles riots related to the Rodney King incident. Although it lasted only five days, the Detroit riot

185

left a deadly toll and vast destruction from looting, arson, and assault. Forty-three people were killed, almost twelve hundred were wounded, more than seven thousand were arrested, and arsonists torched some two thousand buildings. President Johnson ordered U.S. Army and National Guard troops to intervene.

I was in the middle of the riot, not by choice but by happenstance. Billy was on another of his binges, and I had come to the point where I refused to be a passive observer to his shenanigans. I determined to follow him to catch him in the act with women or to drag him out of bars. It has been well said that desperate times require desperate measures. We had a baby to take care of, I was pregnant, and our marriage was on the rocks. My left leg was very sore, almost too sore to walk, but something had to be done.

The troops had imposed a curfew of which I was unaware. I woke a neighbor to babysit Hunter and set out at midnight, well past the 8:00 p.m. curfew, to see if I could find Billy. I knew the streets were dangerous, but I was ready for war and needed to get on with it. I slipped a butcher knife up my sleeve before stepping out into the night. There were fires all over Detroit, and the air was rancid with smoke. The streets, however, were empty of people. Not one person was in sight. Suddenly, a chill went through my body.

"Halt, or I'll shoot!" The voice came from somewhere on a rooftop. I continued walking, not thinking that the voice was shouting at me.

"Halt! Stay where you are, young lady! Put your hands up!" Since I was the only young lady desperate enough to be on the street alone in the middle of the night in a riot zone, I obeyed immediately, abandoning any further thought of my mission. It was very frightening.

Almost instantly, several armed National Guard troops surrounded me and quickly escorted me into the doorway of a storefront. Fortunately, they did not frisk me, or they would have found the butcher knife.

"What do you think you're doing out here?" demanded one of the soldiers. "There's a sniper in the area. You might have been killed. Do you live around here?"

"Yes, just around the corner. I'm looking for my husband."

"Well, look some other time. Go home! That's an order!"

I had no choice. I walked home nervously looking for snipers and thankful for the soldiers.

Daybreak came and Billy still had not come home. The curfew ended at 6:00 a.m. My anger at Billy was not relieved by a restless night. All I could think of was getting satisfaction for the fury that was raging within me. Hunter was still fast asleep, but I would never leave him alone, so I woke the neighbor lady again to keep watch for me while I went on my mission. She understood my dilemma, since she had husband problems of her own. I hid the butcher knife one more time and headed in the direction of a bar where I thought Billy might be. The troops were still very much present, but this time they did not stop me.

I walked as briskly as possible toward my target, the adrenalin rush masking the pain in my leg. I was too focused on being the source of pain for Billy to be concerned about my own. I was pumped by the time I reached my destination.

I found Billy at one of the neighborhood beer joints on Jefferson Avenue. He was sitting at the bar sandwiched between two *sharmutas* (an Arabic word for whores). For millenniums, Arabs have been known for launching raids against merchant caravans or enemies. Surprise attacks are in their blood, and my Arabic blood was boiling. Seeing Billy at the bar infuriated me. Fortunately, in the heat of the moment, I forgot about the butcher knife and instead went straight for the meat of the sandwich. It would have been so easy, albeit cowardly, to stab Billy in the back. Instead, I grabbed Billy by the hair and jerked him off his barstool. He hit the floor hard.

The *sharmutas* had looks of surprise and horror on their faces as Billy hit the floor. They saw that I was filled with rage and probably thought that I would attack them next. Billy was completely stunned. He remained on the floor for a few seconds and then got up slowly. Oddly enough, probably out of embarrassment in front of his lady friends, he did not counterattack. Macho males are not supposed to fight with women, at least not in public.

"*Let's go outside,*" he snarled sharply.

"*Let's go home!*" I demanded.

Billy grabbed me by the arm (fortunately not the one with the knife) and escorted me outside. He easily overpowered me, even in his pickled state. There were only a few cars parked there, and the lot was completely void of people. We were all alone. Billy led me to an open space beyond the cars. Suddenly, he pushed me away, reached into his pocket, and pulled out a pistol. He pointed the pistol at me at point blank range. He could not have been more than six feet away from me.

"This'll be the last time you follow me," he growled. He was very drunk. "I'm going to kill you."

What happened next can only be described as miraculous. Billy pulled the trigger five times. Five bullets whizzed past me. It was over in three seconds. After he fired the last shot, Billy was clearly stone cold sober, but he could not move. He was petrified and absolutely dumbfounded that I was still standing. He just stood there staring at me with his mouth open.

The *sharmutas* at the bar must have called the police when Billy took me outside, because Detroit's finest were there almost as soon as the echo of the last shot had died away. They arrested Billy and took him to jail. I had not just dodged a bullet. I dodged five of them without even moving a muscle! Only God's protection can explain the fact that I am still alive.

It seems incredible to me now in hindsight, but despite the attempt on my life, I did not leave Billy. I had him released from jail, and for a few weeks we coexisted. I was in my third month of pregnancy when the shooting incident occurred. In another few weeks, I would be hospitalized. My life would be threatened one more time. I simply did not know when to leave.

Breakaway

But ultimately, that's not all.
The time will come when you must fall
And give your life unselfishly—
A perfect immolation.

House of Pain

*T*HREE WEEKS DRAGGED BY, AND I WAS NOT getting better. I was still bruised all over, and my left calf was very swollen from Billy's kick. The Detroit riots had come and gone, and I was still weak with a fever. I thought I might be catching a summer cold, but what did that have to do with my leg hurting so much? It was increasingly difficult for me to walk. I took care of Hunter and made sure he was fed and changed. He was always my main concern; I could endure anything as long as no one hurt him. I felt so alone. I had no family or friends nearby, and, of course, my family surely would not have helped me anyway, since my parents had disowned me.

My cousin Marilee gave me an open invitation to find refuge with her, but she was not happy with her marriage either. Even so, disgusted with Billy and afraid of more beatings, I had packed the trunk of the car twice with a few belongings and driven over to Marilee's for safe haven. However, Billy always came after me, begging me to forgive him, and promising that he would change and stop drinking. I always gave in.

My illness was getting worse every day. The excruciating pain increased beyond my threshold to bear it. I could not understand why the fever persisted. It was not anything like I had experienced before. My left leg was getting bigger each day, so that it was more and more difficult to get out of bed. Another week passed, and I was constantly crying for help. Billy and his mother took care of Hunter now, but they neglected to care for me. I wanted them to take care of him. I simply was unable to do it.

One day, a little over a month after the kicking incident, Billy came into the apartment drunk. He wanted money for more beer. We were flat broke. He asked for my wedding band so he could pawn it and get a few dollars. I refused to give it to him. That was the wrong thing to do. I was lying in bed with no one around to help me, and I spoke without thinking.

Billy approached the bed and threatened me: "Give me that ring, or I'll kill you right now." He punched me in the face, and my lip started to bleed. I took off the band and threw it at him. *"Take it, and don't come back. I hate you!"*

Billy literally ran out the door with the ring in hand. He could not wait to get to the pawnshop. A complete invalid now, I contemplated the stark reality that Billy's beer had become more important than our marriage. The symbolism was profound. My ring was gone. The marriage was gone. Why was I still hanging around?

I did something in that moment of questioning that I had not done in a long while. In utter desperation, I cried out to God: "Dear God, please help me get out of here. Please help me."

The pain escalated, and two days later my right leg began to swell also. I was suffering beyond anything I had ever felt. I knew that I could no longer deal with it. It was time to get some help.

When Billy returned, I demanded that he take me to the emergency room. He called a taxi and carried me outside. I could not put weight on my legs; they were both swollen to twice normal size. I was moaning from the pain as we got into the taxi. The taxi driver took one look at me and sped off.

At the emergency room, Billy had to carry me until he found a wheelchair. When the nurses saw the condition of my legs, they knew immediately what was wrong. They rushed me onto a gurney. I was immediately given heparin and painkillers. The emergency room doctor said that I had a deep vein thrombosis—a blood clot—in my left leg, and it had traveled to the right leg.

"How long have you been hurting?" asked the doctor.

"About a month, maybe five weeks," I answered tearfully.

"How did this happen?" I believe he already knew the answer.

"I was kicked," I said, glancing at Billy.

"You're one lucky girl," he explained. "It's amazing that the blood clot traveled through your system to the other leg without stopping in your heart or lungs. If it had, you would not be alive now. It's obvious that God loves you. He must have something special for you to do." He had compassion written all over him.

The doctor told Billy to go and register me for admittance to the hospital. Billy jumped at the order, as the doctor did not hide his disgust with him for assaulting me. They kept me in the emergency room until they were satisfied that I could be moved to a private room. Billy, meanwhile, had returned and was sitting humbly beside my bed holding my hand. He was very dejected, obviously guilt-ridden for the condition I was in.

"Billy, what about Hunter, who will take care of him while I'm in the hospital?" I missed him so much already.

"Mom will take him."

"Okay," I said hesitantly, but I was not happy about it.

I had no choice. My family and I were not on speaking terms yet. I wanted them to accept me the way I was and for whom I married, but they refused. So, regretfully, Hunter went to Billy's mother. I prayed that he would be all right.

The days in the hospital turned into weeks and the weeks into three months. I was very discouraged. My spirits were lifted only occasionally when Hunter was brought to see me. He looked so handsome in his yellow pajamas and sandy hair. Hunter was growing so much! Sadly, I was not able to be with him, to care for him, but my mother-in-law was good to him. At least that was of some comfort to me.

The pain was continuous, and the medicines I was taking were not helping. Near the end of the third month, one of the doctors entered my room and gave me two choices.

"The blood clots are not responding to our treatments," he explained. "We have to advise you that you must make a very difficult decision. You have two options. One is to abort the baby in order to save your own life."

"There's no way I'll abort my baby," I replied immediately. I was almost through my second trimester by then, and the baby was kicking up a storm already. "I won't kill my baby. What's my other option?"

"You can decide to keep the baby and continue with the treatments. In that case, there's a real possibility that we might lose both you and the baby." The doctor took my hand sympathetically and waited for my decision.

"How much time do I have?" I asked.

"Not long," he responded.

"I'm twenty years old, and you're asking me to make this decision for my life and my baby's life? I can't lose my baby. I won't do it." I sank into my pillow and began to cry. I asked to be alone.

I never for one second contemplated aborting my baby. I recalled the emotional agony I had experienced with the illegal abortion and knew that I would not do it. More than that, I felt my baby moving. He was a living, growing baby. How could I take his life? I would rather have given up my own life to save his, but I was not given that choice. I refused to even think about the abortion option.

I did not know what to do, but I remembered to pray. I recalled that day when I asked Christ into my heart. I remembered that he loved me and died for me. I remembered the promise of his presence and that he would answer me if I prayed to him. I had not grown as a Christian nor had I read the Bible, but I still believed in Jesus as my Savior. I prayed a very simple little prayer: "Dear Jesus, please help me. I don't know what to do."

For two days, I pondered the weight of my decision to trust the treatments, not knowing if they would work, but confident that I had chosen rightly to spare my baby's life. On the third day, a visitor came to my room. His name was Ed Lorry. He taught a Sunday school class at Temple Baptist where I became a Christian. He was in his late fifties and had a very quiet, gentle manner. He brought a beautiful bouquet of roses from the congregation. It touched my heart. I had not been to Temple or talked with anyone from the church since my conversion. Still, the people there cared enough to send flowers. Ed said that my aunt Grace told them about my illness. After some congenial small talk, Ed came to the point of his visit.

"Nadia, may I ask you a question?"

"Of course, Ed."

"Do you believe that Jesus can heal you if you ask him?"

"Yes, I believe he can, but I haven't been much of a Christian. I haven't been to church . . ."

Ed interrupted my self-denigration. "His love is not limited to what you do, Nadia. Remember our study in Romans. He loved us while we were still hostile to him, even while we were his enemies as unbelievers. He loved the Apostle Paul before he became a believer, while he was actively persecuting the church. No, his love is not measured by how good you've been, Nadia. God's love is not measured by how often you go to church."

Tears flooded my eyes and began to stream down my face. "I've been sick for so long, Ed. The doctors don't know what to do. I had to decide between losing my baby or risking the loss of my own life and the baby's life. I can't kill my baby. I'd rather die in his place." I was sobbing so hard that I could not go on.

"God's strength is in our weakness, Nadia. That's when he can work miracles. It sounds like you need a miracle."

"Oh yes! I miss my little boy, Hunter, so very much, and my baby is kicking inside me. I want to go home. I don't know what to do, Ed. I want to be healed." I meant it with all my heart.

"Nadia, if you believe that God can heal you, then let's ask him to do it. If you have faith to believe it, he will not disappoint you. God loves you. Love never disappoints."

Ed came to the bedside and took my hand. He asked me to bow my head as he prayed. There weren't any bells and whistles. There was no show. A simple man of God took my hand and prayed for my healing. In childlike faith, I agreed with his prayer. When he finished, he said in a kind and gentle way, "Rest now, Nadia, God is with you. He has never left you. Just trust him. He has a plan for your life. He has something great for you to do. You're his child, and you're very special to him."

And that was it. Ed Lorry, the simple Sunday school teacher from Temple Baptist Church left the room without a single bit of fanfare. He left behind a pregnant woman too sick to stand for three months. I waved to him as he went out the door. "Thank you, Ed, thank you for coming. It means the world to me."

I looked at my legs. There was no change. They were still swollen. I still felt the pain of my condition unmasked by the medication. I still could not get out of bed, but I knew somehow that I was not the same person that Ed came to visit. The heavy load of care that I had been bearing for months was gone. I felt completely free of it. I knew in my heart that I would be healed and that I would have two boys to take care of. I just did not know when.

From you a host of things will be,
But in the meantime be a tree,
And leave your destiny to me—
God's final declaration.

The Miracle

THE NEXT MORNING I WOKE UP AND INSTANTLY noticed a change. The pain that I had grown so accustomed to was gone. I wiggled my toes. There was no pain. I moved my right leg, then my left. There was no pain. I pulled the bed sheet back and looked at my legs. They both had gone back to their normal size! I suddenly felt an urge, no, more than an urge. I felt a force pushing me forward, pushing me out of bed. I did not know at the time that it was the Holy Spirit. I would not understand that until later. I gently swung my body around to the edge of the bed. With caution and a little fear, I placed my left foot on the floor. I had no pain! I put the other foot down. No pain! I stood on both feet for the first time in months and began to walk.

"*I have no pain! I have no pain!*" I shouted.

I ran out to the nurses' station yelling, "*I have no pain! I have no pain!*" The nurses dropped what they were doing and ran over to me. They examined my legs. They saw me walking and jumping. They were incredulous.

"Yesterday I couldn't get out of bed. Today I have no pain!" I was so excited.

Two doctors who had treated me came out of rooms to see what the commotion was all about. They just stood there with their mouths open when they saw me.

Finally, one of the nurses asked, "Nadia, what happened to you? How did this happen? You have no pain?"

"No pain," I replied, "and look, my legs are normal again."

I told them that Ed Lorry, the kind and gentle man from Temple Baptist, had come to visit me the day before and prayed with me for healing. I did not understand very well how to tell them about the miracle from Jesus. I was a new Christian and did not know yet what to say, but I told them the best I could. They were all amazed and very happy for me. Tears of joy were running down their cheeks.

I returned to my room and had only been there a few minutes when my doctor came to examine me. He took some blood and said the lab would read the findings right away. In less than an hour, he was back. He said I could go home in three days. In the meantime, they had to measure my leg and make elastic stockings that I would have to wear for the rest of my life. He explained that the stockings would help to promote circulation in my legs. It sounded like a good idea to me.

Three days later when the promised stockings arrived, I took one look at them and almost went into orbit: "I can't wear those ugly things. There's no way I'm going to do it." They were thick and flesh-colored and went up past my knees. I imagined being called granny all my life.

"Well, you have no choice," the doctor said, half smiling at my vain reaction. "They'll help to prevent any future blood clots. It won't be so bad, once you get used to them."

"When can I go home?" I asked impatiently. He could see that I was avoiding any more talk about the stockings.

"This afternoon, as soon as the paperwork is ready. We'll call your husband to pick you up, and you're on your way, young lady."

"Thank you, Dr. Morgan." I gave him a kiss on the cheek to show him how happy I was to go home. "Thank you for everything you've done."

He smiled and said, "You're welcome, but it's pretty obvious that God did what we couldn't do. Now go home, take care of yourself and your babies, and don't let anyone hurt you again."

As soon as he said that, I made up my mind to never be a victim again. Right there in front of Dr. Morgan, I took my stand and said, "Don't worry, this will never happen to me again. Things will be different from now on."

Billy picked me up and brought Hunter with him at my request. I had to see him and hold him close to me. Hunter ran to me with open arms. My baby had grown so much! It was like heaven holding him again. How I missed my baby! Now I could take care of him again and give him all my love. I kissed him over and over, and he returned hugs and kisses for me.

Billy was also thrilled to finally have me back home. It seemed that he was going to change and try to be a better husband. He was lonely at home, and he had a lot of guilt over what he had done to me. The thought of losing his baby and me caused him to stop drinking. Yes, he stopped drinking, but it was not for long.

Billy was doing fine until his mother and sister interfered. He was beginning to rise above their level when they brought him back down with a six-pack of beer. One day, I found them drinking together on his mother's back porch. He was too weak to resist. It was incredible to me that they could be so ignorant, knowing full well that only negative consequences could follow from their actions.

As I was leaving them, we talked about Hunter. "What a wonderful baby he is," they said. "He was so easy to care for when you were in the hospital." I agreed wholeheartedly and thanked them for their help. At the same time, I wondered how Hunter would turn out if he were to be raised by Billy's mother. Would he turn out just like his father? I imagined Hunter as an alcoholic and a wife beater, and my heart became very sad. That would never happen! How unfortunate that Billy was raised as he was! His family never gave him a chance. I determined to keep Hunter and my new baby away from bad influences for as long as I lived.

The Christmas holidays came and went. Billy found a job at a factory about two miles from our apartment. He was making small auto parts for one of the Big Three and was working every day. He was a good worker when he was sober. We had a little extra cash. I received two thousand dollars from the hospital for overpayment by my insurance companies, more money than I had ever owned at one time. We needed a new car, so I bought a used Chevy. I replaced the old TV, and there was still enough money left over for groceries and stocking the pantry. Life was good, better than ever.

I needed a few things for the new baby, so I bundled Hunter up for the January cold and packed him into the Chevy. What a sweet child he was! He was a toddler now at nineteen months. While we were at the store, I began to feel some pain. I decided it would be best to return home in case I went into labor. I was due any day.

The pains became sharper and more regular. It was time. I called Billy at work: "It's my time, Billy, hurry home. *It's my time! The baby is on his way!*" Billy was there in less than fifteen minutes. "You need to take me to the hospital, *now!*" I screamed as the pains were increasing. Billy picked Hunter up and took me by the arm. We raced to the hospital.

Today it is called Hutzel Hospital, but in the sixties it was Women's Hospital of Detroit. I was rushed into a room while Billy filled out all the admission and insurance forms. Four hours passed and my labor pains were severe, but not as severe as they were with Hunter. With his birth, I thought I would die. Between contractions, I mused about Hunter's birth and how it transformed my life.

Suddenly, my thoughts were interrupted by the reality of the moment. "Nurse! Help me! Nurse!" The pain was excruciating. "My baby is coming!" The nurse checked, and sure enough, the baby's head was showing. They whisked me off to the delivery room, and I gave birth to a beautiful baby boy. My miracle boy! We named him Ryan. He had thick, black hair, just as his brother did when he was born. It was long, almost touching his shoulders. He had beautiful olive-colored skin. He was perfectly healthy. He weighed seven pounds and eight ounces and was nineteen-and-a-half inches tall. I was in labor for only five-and-a-half hours. It was so great to hold him in my arms. I was overcome with emotion. I was escorted back to my room, while Ryan was taken to the nursery.

Billy was waiting in the room for me. He was anxious to see Ryan, so he went to the nursery right away. He came back wearing a happy smile and swaggering. He was awed by how beautiful Ryan was. It was a happy time for us.

I could not wait for Hunter to see his new baby brother. I was kept in the hospital for three days; that was the minimum at the time. Finally, it was time to go home. Hunter was so excited. "Baby, baby," he said, pointing at his brother and giggling. He kissed Ryan's cheek and wanted to hold him. "Not now, Hunter, when Mommy is in bed, okay?" Still tired from my ordeal, I made a beeline to the bed as soon as we got home. I cuddled with Ryan, and Hunter climbed up on the bed with us. He lay next to Ryan and caressed him with his little hand.

I lay there quietly with my two babies, thinking about my life. What if I had listened to the doctors who had given me the option of aborting Ryan? What if a gentle and kind man had not come to pray with me? What if I had not been healed? What if God did not love me? I snuggled close to my two babies with a full heart and began to cry softly. They were tears of pure joy! I was healed! I was in heaven!

And one more thing: I never wore those ugly, horrid-looking stockings!

Breakaway

Despite our best attempts to gain
The freedom that will keep us sane,
There always comes another time
For utter aggravation.

King Arthur's Club

TWO MONTHS PASSED, AND WE HAD TO MOVE again. I found a little bungalow on West Vernor Highway near Lonyo Street, close to the Norfolk Southern Railroad tracks.

I came to know the train schedule by heart. Freight was moved during the day, of course, but trains came frequently during the night as well. The whistles always woke me, and the rumble of the heavy-laden cars caused the bungalow to vibrate gradually until it shook all over like a dog coming out of the water. When the train passed, the bungalow would lie down again and rest quietly, waiting for the next train.

It was not a pleasant place to live, but it was all we could afford. It was very small: two tiny bedrooms, a living room, an almost microscopic kitchen, and the bath. It had a basement, too, which looked like it belonged in a horror movie. I never went there. It spooked me. It reminded me of Sylvia's basement. I made sure the basement door was always locked.

Breakaway

Billy still was not responsible enough to keep a job, and, as usual, we were broke. I had to find work to feed my babies. I was only twenty years old, but my twenty-first birthday was coming up in May.

I got a job at Sarjanian Glove Factory near the house. It was an interesting job—for a short while. I made waterproof latex gloves. I operated the machine that dipped cloth work gloves into a vat that coated them with latex. They were dyed gloves: pretty reds, yellows, greens, and blues. I had to quit after two months. Things at home got rougher, and I did not want my sister-in-law babysitting my children anymore. I was not making much money anyway. I needed more money, so I continued looking for a job and a new sitter.

I got hired at Allied Paper Company making paper plates, but that didn't last long either. Very soon I got bored. It was hard to stay focused on making plates, since Billy was causing problems at home, as usual, plus I was working too hard for the money I made. I had to quit. Getting another job was always easy for me. Keeping it was the hard part.

Next, I found a job at King Arthur's Club, an upscale nightclub that has long since been demolished. I was walking on Schaefer Road, window-shopping, when I saw the building and became curious about what was inside. The doors were huge and ornate with gorgeous carvings, like those on a castle. I was intrigued and had to satisfy my curiosity, so I opened the door and poked my head inside.

"Come on in," said a deep voice whose owner was concealed in the dimly lit room.

"Come on in," it repeated, "we won't bite you."

I stepped inside nervously, not knowing what to expect.

"Wow," said the voice, "you sure are beautiful. What's your name?

"Nadia," I said uneasily, despite the friendliness of the voice.

"You don't need to be nervous. My name is Jay Hernandez. I'm the night manager for the club. How old are you?"

Breakaway

I was still trying to adjust to the darkness, and then I saw him more clearly as I stepped farther into the room. Jay was tending bar. He was a tall man, very husky, with jet-black hair, thick eyebrows, a big, black mustache, and a beautiful, white smile. Several men and women were drinking at the bar.

"I'm twenty, why?" I asked.

"Too bad," he responded, "if you were twenty-one, I'd hire you as a cocktail waitress."

"What's a cocktail waitress?" I asked naively.

"What! You must be kidding, right?" he answered.

"No, I've never heard of a cocktail waitress. What's a cocktail?" He was amazed at how green I was.

"Okay, let me show you," he said, pointing to a young woman wearing black pants and a white blouse. "She's a cocktail waitress. She prepares and serves drinks to our customers."

"Oh," I said, "that sounds easy."

"I'll hire you if you don't tell anyone that you're only twenty. When will you be twenty-one?"

"In one month," I replied, excited about working again.

"Great! You're hired!" He was genuinely enthusiastic.

"Wait, I don't have a car. I can't work here. It's too far from home. I took a bus over here today, but I don't want to do that every day," I objected with obvious disappointment.

"Where do you live?" Jay asked.

"I live on Lonyo and West Vernor Highway."

"Oh, that's not far. I'll take you home if you can find a way here," Jay offered.

"Okay," I said, "how much will I get paid?"

He was jubilant. "I'll start you at a dollar fifty an hour and you keep all your tips. You're so pretty, you'll make a lot in tips. Don't worry. Come into my office. I'll show you the uniform."

He took me to his office and pulled out a teeny, micro-mini, black skirt.

"Oh, my God! What's that?" I shrieked.

He laughed heartily and said, "It's your uniform."

"I can't wear that. It's too short. My husband would kill me if he saw me in that!"

"It's not as bad as you think," Jay explained. "You wear the skirt with black, mesh stockings and a white blouse. You'll look absolutely sexy. Oh, you'll be wearing black, high heels, too."

"Well, I don't know," I hesitated. "The waitress out front was fully clothed. I thought that was the uniform."

"That's the uniform for days. I need someone at night. This is the night uniform. Come on," he said, "no one is going to bother you. It's only a uniform, and all the girls wear it."

"Okay," I said out of desperation, "I'll try it."

"That's the spirit. I'll see you tomorrow night at 9:00. You'll work until we close at 2:00 a.m."

I told Billy the good news as soon as I got home. He was angry that I was not home earlier, but when I told him about being hired as a cocktail waitress, he really got fired up. My news was a stick in a hornet's nest.

"You can't work there," he ordered. "You need to stay home and take care of me."

"We need the money, Billy. I wouldn't do it if you had a better job, but I really don't have much choice."

"I'll get a better job tomorrow."

"No, you won't."

"You're not going to be a cocktail waitress!" He yelled as though I were across town, compensating in volume for his inability to persuade me rationally.

It was useless to argue, so I said nothing. I slept on the sofa that night. I woke up around midnight to find Billy gone. I checked on the babies to make sure they were asleep, got out of my clothes, and slipped into bed. I did not care where Billy was.

In the morning, I called the manager at King Arthur's to let him know that I would not be coming to work.

"The job's here for you any time you change your mind," he said. "I won't be hiring anyone else right now."

I thanked him for the opportunity.

A few days went by, and things were getting tougher. Money for food was running low. I did not know what to do. Billy was still working only sporadically, and whatever money he earned all but disappeared before it hit my hands. I had to do something. I had to work.

One night Billy disappeared again. I never knew when he would be home, but I had learned to read the signs, and this time I expected him to be gone for days. I called my neighbor and asked her to babysit for me. She was more than willing to help me. Then I called Jay Hernandez.

"Jay, this is Nadia, I'd like to come to work tonight. Is that all right with you?"

"Come on in. I'll be waiting for you. Take a taxi and I'll pay for it when you get here."

I said thanks, grabbed my purse, and called a Yellow Cab. At the club, Jay paid for the cab as he said he would, and I went straight to the dressing room to change into my uniform. I was not prepared for what happened next.

Dressed in my new outfit (or what there was of it), I walked out into the club, and all the men whistled and applauded, "Look at that body!" a man exclaimed.

"I knew you'd look sexy. Look at those sexy legs!" Jay looked like he was going to come out of his shoes.

"Okay, Jay," I said officially, "what do I do?"

"This is Sherry," he replied. "She'll train you. Just follow her, and do what she does."

Sherry was a pro. She knew every drink and every mix under the sun. I was confused. I had no idea there were so many different drinks: Tom Collins, Bloody Mary, Green Dragon, Screwdriver, Hardball Cooler, Black Russian, Old Fashioned, Rob Roy, Godfather, and the list went on and on. I only knew about Budweiser beer, since that is what Billy always drank. I followed Sherry like an obedient puppy. I was utterly lost without her.

One evening, after I had been at the club for about a week, two men came up to me and asked for a Tom Collins each. I proudly prepared their drinks and served them, noticing that they were dressed alike with black tuxedos, white shirts, and bow ties.

"Here you go, gentlemen, are you guys twins?" I asked coyly.

"Why do you ask?" They looked at each other in disbelief and smiled at me.

"Because you're dressed alike," I said innocently.

They turned and looked at each other, smiling ear to ear. They were really amused. Had they heard right?

They said they were members of the band. I had been so busy for a week that I had not even noticed the band. They were both very cute. The shorter one had dark hair and a mustache. He looked like Neil Diamond. He introduced himself as "Little Bo." I could not have imagined at the time that some day I would marry him and stay married for twelve years. That is a whole other story.

"My name's Dave," the other one said. He was tall with light brown hair and blue eyes. "I play the trumpet. Bo is the drummer in the band. What's your name?"

"Nadia," I replied to the twins. I told them that I used to watch Dick Clark's *American Bandstand* on TV when I was younger. Little Bo said he played on *American Bandstand* with *Johnny and the Hurricanes*. I was shocked.

"Oh yes! I remember them," I said. I really was not too sure about that, but I thought the name sounded familiar. Their current band was called *Jamie Coe and the Gigolos*. I did not know what a gigolo was, and I was afraid to ask.

"Well, we have to get back for another set," Little Bo said, "so listen this time, and watch when you can." I said I would.

The band sounded great, but Little Bo was staring at me from the stage and smiling at me all night long. I knew I was in trouble. I finished my shift and waited for Jay to take me home.

"You're doing a great job. I'm proud of you," he said as he was driving. "Come and sit next to me, I won't bite you."

"No, Jay, please just take me home." He grabbed my arm and pulled me over to his side. "Now, sit here and just let me hold your hand," he insisted. I was scared. What was going to happen to me?

"Kiss me in the ear," he said sternly.

"No," I said, trying to get free.

"Just once, okay, and I'll leave you alone."

"*No!*" I tried to get away from him, and he pulled me back. "Jay, I thought you were decent. Why are you doing this?"

"Just give me one kiss and I'll leave you alone," he demanded.

"I won't, Jay, it's wrong." He became angry and was silent, but he let me go. When he stopped at a red light, I quickly opened the door and jumped out. I was not familiar with the area, but I was terrified that Jay would do something to harm me. I could feel the adrenalin pumping. I had to survive this ordeal. I had two babies to care for.

Jay followed me slowly with the car. I kept walking as calmly as I could, trying to be strong. "Nadia, get back in the car," he demanded.

"*No,*" I screamed back at him.

"I promise I won't bother you. It's after two o'clock and there are a lot of crazy guys out here. You'll get killed or raped. Get in the car. I won't be responsible if anything happens to you. Please get in the car. I won't do anything. I'll just take you home. Now come on, Nadia," he pleaded.

"Do you promise?" I asked firmly.

"Yes, I promise," he said.

After ten minutes of haggling with Jay, I finally got back into the car, but I was glued to the door with my hand on the handle, ready to jump if I had to.

He kept his promise.

The seasons come, the seasons go,
The challenges of life we know,
But in the end we take our stand
With rising aspiration.

It's Over

BILLY RETURNED ABOUT EIGHT O'CLOCK IN THE morning. He had been out carousing all night with his sister. He was walking with a limp, staggering from side to side, still noticeably drunk. I was in the kitchen preparing breakfast for my babies.

"I neeess sssome mmonnney," he said, slurring his words.

"Why do you need money?" I asked.

"I need a ssssisss-pack," he stammered.

"What! You've been out drinking all night and you want the last five dollars I have? I'm going to use this money to buy milk for Hunter and Ryan. The answer is no. I don't have money for beer." I was livid.

Billy was furious. Hunter was in his high chair eating his cereal, and Ryan was in his crib waiting for his milk bottle. Billy snatched the bottle from me, removed the cap and nipple, and poured the milk into the sink. Hunter was half finished with his cereal. Billy took the bowl away from him and poured the contents into the sink. I looked on in horror and disbelief.

He had the guts to say, "If I can't have my beer, they can't eat!" I attacked him with the fury of a mother bear separated from her cubs, clawing, scratching, ripping, and tearing at him with all my strength.

"Those are your children, you idiot," I screamed. "What's the matter with you? Your beer is more important than your children! I hate you! Get out! I don't want you here anymore. You can beat me, and you can try to kill me, but you're not going to hurt my babies! *Get out! Get out, and stay out!"* He left, and I thought it was over.

Drunk as he was, Billy was not finished. He came back and began to hit me in the face and punch me in the stomach. Then he snatched an empty beer bottle from the trash and hit me on the head with it. He almost knocked me out. Dizzy and weak, my knees collapsed, and I fell to the floor crying, "Leave us alone. Go away. Please, go away. Please, God, make him go away." I had no more strength to fight. I barely had enough strength to speak. I believe God mercifully heard that prayer. Billy left again, and I immediately picked up the phone and called the police.

I managed somehow to prepare the last of the formula I had in the refrigerator and give it to Ryan. He went to sleep immediately after I fed him. Both he and Hunter were wonderful sleepers. I gave Hunter his toys and tried to comfort him. He was very nervous after seeing me beaten. I held him closely for a long time. "Everything will be all right, sweetheart," I said, "Mommy is okay."

In a short while, there was a knock at the door. The police had arrived. I told them what happened. They could see that I was badly beaten.

One of the officers looked at me sadly and said, "I'm sorry, ma'am, there's really nothing we can do. We can't interfere with husband and wife domestic problems. We don't have jurisdiction in these matters. I'm so sorry."

"*What!*" I was flabbergasted. "What do you mean? My husband beat me again and almost killed me, and you say you can't do anything to him?"

"I'm sorry, ma'am, that's correct," he explained. "The law says we can't step in. It's a violation of your husband's rights. It's a family matter. We can't step in unless . . ."

"Unless what?" I interrupted. "Unless he kills me?"

"That's right, ma'am, then it's a case of homicide. That we can deal with. It's the law."

"There's one other option," said the other officer.

"What's that?" I asked sarcastically, "I kill him before he kills me?"

"No, ma'am, but you can leave him before it's too late, before he harms you further or harms your babies. There's no law saying you can't leave your husband, ma'am." They took another look at my swollen, bloodstained face and body, shook their heads sadly, and wished me good luck.

"Thank you, officers," I said, "I understand that it's out of your hands." I just could not believe it. How could this be? What was I to do? I did not want a divorce. I loved Billy. I thought it was love anyway. I was so confused. Why did he have to drink and beat me and go with women? Why couldn't I just have a nice life for a change? If I were alone, what would happen to my babies? I had no money. I had lived three years of hell, and things were getting worse all the time. I needed to do something quickly. I needed to leave.

I really wanted to leave, but where could I go? My parents had disowned me and wanted nothing to do with me. Occasionally, they would call and ask about my children. Should I call them and ask for help, just this once? I decided that it would not hurt to try. My mother answered the phone, and I told her everything that had happened. I told her that I was going to leave Billy. My parents talked it over, and my father agreed to help me move my personal things and the TV I had bought.

I did not own a suitcase. I packed my clothes and the babies' clothes in two cardboard boxes and some paper bags.

Later in the day, I took Hunter and Ryan for a walk. Ryan was in the stroller, while I took Hunter's hand. We all needed the fresh air, and I needed the time to think about what to do next.

It was decided for me once again. While I was away, Billy came home and found that I had packed to leave. He decided to take the TV and sell it in order to buy beer. When I returned with the children, Billy and the TV were gone.

I felt a steady anger bubbling up within myself until it reached the boiling point. How could he have taken my TV, the very one I bought with the insurance money from the hospital? Did he really think that he could benefit from putting me in the hospital? I steeled my mind to get the TV back. It was not about the TV. It was about me. This was the last straw. It took only a few seconds to formulate my plan.

I called a friend to come and stay with Hunter and Ryan, while I went on a manhunt. Where would he take my TV? I kept a 38 Special under my mattress since crazy Leon had threatened my life. I loaded the pistol with five bullets and headed for Billy's sister's house. I knew he would take the TV there. I was not going to be cheated, nor was I ever going to be beaten again! I walked the two blocks to Susie's house determined to even the score.

Susie lived with her husband and two children in a third floor apartment. I took the elevator and knocked on her door, hoping to see Billy. I was disappointed. Susie opened the door.

"Hi, Susie," I said calmly, "is Billy here? I need to talk to him."

"No, Nadia," she replied, "I haven't seen him."

I knew in my gut that she was lying. "That's interesting," I said, "I've looked everywhere for him except here. I was sure I'd find him here."

"Well, I'm sorry, honey," she said with a straight face, "he ain't here."

"Are you sure?" I asked more forcefully.

"I said he ain't, didn't I?" Her voice said one thing, but her face told the truth. She looked like a liar to me.

"Okay then, if you see him, tell him that he needs to return my TV to the house or else. Will you tell him that?" I looked her straight in the eyes.

"Yeah, I'll tell him," she said with a smile, but I noticed a hint of concern on her face. All the abuse I had suffered made me an expert in reading people.

Susie closed the door, and I pretended to take the staircase instead of the elevator. I slammed the door to the staircase loud enough so it could be heard inside Susie's apartment. I waited a couple of minutes behind the door; then I opened it quietly and tiptoed back to Susie's door. It had a huge keyhole to accommodate a skeleton key. I could easily look through it and see who was in her living room. I took a good, long look at Billy, sitting smugly on the sofa like a king, watching *my* TV. He had a big grin on his face, like he had just won the lottery.

I fingered the gun in my purse and knocked on the door.

"Billy, you can come out now. I know you're in there. Open the door."

There was no response.

"*Billy, I saw you through the keyhole. Come out of there now!*" I banged on the door with the butt of the pistol.

Susie opened it, and I quickly stepped inside. Billy emerged from the closet looking very sheepish.

"Billy, I need to talk to you privately. Let's step outside."

He followed me into the hallway.

"Now, Billy, listen carefully. I want you to go in there and get my TV right now and carry it back to the house. I can't take it anymore. I've had it with you." I pulled the gun out of my purse and pointed it at his head. "Do it now, or I'll shoot! I'll wait here!"

The blood drained from Billy's face until it was as white as his tee shirt. Suddenly he was an albino puppy dog. He put his tail between his legs and sulked back into the living room. Seconds later, he appeared with my TV.

"Good," I said, "now walk in front of me, and be careful. If you drop it, I'll shoot you in the back. Let's take the stairs."

Breakaway

Billy started down the stairs gingerly. I was right behind him with the pistol pointed at his back. He believed that I would shoot him if he dropped it. I know that he was never more certain of anything in his life. Beads of perspiration were building up around his neck, and he was trembling. We reached the ground floor and headed down the street.

Billy was silent. He was walking very carefully. The short walk gave me the opportunity to say some things I had kept on my mind for a very long time. I had a captive audience!

"Billy, don't talk. Just listen," I said with authority. Billy said nothing. "I'm going to tell you once and for all, it's over. I want you out of my life, and I never want to see your face again. That means I also never want you to see your children's faces again. Now you can have all the beer and women you want. I've taken everything that I'm going to take from you. I'll never take another beating. I'll never take abuse from you again. We're finished. I've made up my mind. It's over. I'm going to divorce you, and you'll never see me or the children again!"

We marched the rest of the way to our bungalow in silence. Billy carefully set the TV back on its stand. The gun was still pointed at him when he moved cautiously toward the door. I felt in control of my life for the first time since I married Billy. Unfortunately, it had come to this, but I had to make him understand. There was no other way. Billy got the message.

I told him to leave and never come back. I did not know what he would do. Surprisingly, he left without saying a word and returned to his sister's apartment. I began packing what little I owned.

When I finished packing, I called my father to come over with the trailer. Besides the TV, there were only a few pieces of furniture, and they weren't heavy. My father drove off with the trailer. I took Hunter by the hand, lifted Ryan to my hip, and we headed to my car. I did not know where to go or what I was going to do, but I knew I had to break away from my old life and start a new one.

Breakaway

It would be a gross understatement to say that I was short on resources. I had five dollars in cash, no savings, no groceries, and no place to stay. I decided to go to my parents and ask them to let me and my babies stay there for a while until I found a job and was able to pay for an apartment. I knocked on the door of the house I grew up in, the same door I had used a thousand times before. My mother answered and seemed surprised to see me. That was strange to me since my father had just picked up my furniture less than two hours before. I meekly asked her if I could stay there and have my sisters babysit for me while I went out looking for a job.

To my chagrin, she said in Arabic, "No, you can't stay here, Nadia."

"Why not?" I asked. "I have nowhere else to go, and it's only temporary. I won't have trouble finding work."

"No, Nadia. If I let you stay here, your sisters will think that I didn't care about the fact that you married an American. They'll do the same as you and go against your father and me. I don't want them to marry Americans. You can't stay here."

I turned around, picked up my children, and walked away with a broken heart. The pain from my mother's rejection was worse than the pain from my father's beatings. I needed her most just then, and she would not let me in the house.

Breakaway

The morning breaks, a new day starts,
We wake to learn and play new parts.
The past we leave behind us now
For greater approbation.

Go-Go Girl

THE TUXEDO HOTEL WAS CLOSE TO OUR HOUSE. I used to walk past it as a five-year-old to take food to my grandfather. It is ironic that the trail of sexual and physical abuse that started with my grandfather and ended with my leaving Billy made a circular journey from the Dix Hotel to the Tuxedo Hotel, both within a block of each other. It ended almost exactly where it began.

The hotel's clientele were mostly out-of-town, blue-collar workers and truckers. Very seldom did women stay at the Tuxedo; hookers, yes, but usually no others. I knew that it was not elegant, but it was cheap, and it was nearby. I went directly there. I asked the receptionist if she had a room available for my children and me. She looked at the children and then at me: "Are you sure you want to stay here?"

"Yes, I know that families don't usually stay here, but I need a room for just one night. I have nowhere else to go, and all I have is five dollars, just enough for the night. Please, let us stay."

The receptionist looked at my children again and quietly said, "Okay, you can stay tonight."

I was so relieved. "Thank you, thank you," I said over my shoulder, as I took the children up to our room. Hunter and Ryan were hungry and tired. Luckily, I had milk for Ryan and sandwiches for Hunter and me. The room was facing my parent's house. I made my sons comfortable on the bed and went to the window. I stood there looking at the house I had once lived in, wondering how my life had become one of turmoil and despair. I wanted so much to feel loved by my parents. The pain was so deep and intense that it was only a few moments before it took over my entire being. Tears began to flow freely down my cheeks. Sadness and loneliness overwhelmed me.

I stayed at the window for a long time, the pages of the past turning slowly in my memory. It was as though I was looking at the scrapbook of my life, but the pictures were not beautiful. My whole life was a journey through abuse. Finally, it was over, but it had taken its toll. I was very tired, not just superficially, but tired at my core, in my bones. I had made my breakaway, but I was emotionally drained and physically exhausted. I fell on the bed and was about to go to sleep when I realized that we shared the room with other guests. One of them touched my face.

"Oh, my God, there are roaches in here!" I screamed and jumped off the bed. Of course, I woke the babies, so they began to cry. I calmed them down right away and tucked them in tightly in case the roaches came on the bed. Then I went to war.

What an incredible and invincible enemy the roaches were! Like cowards they ran in all directions as soon as I came near them, but they were not cowards really. Running was a tactical feature of their brilliant strategy to retain their territory. The more I chased, the more they ran. I soon realized that I could not conquer them.

I was already bushed before taking on the roaches, so I finally gave up and snuggled with Ryan and Hunter who were both still awake. I assured them that they would be safe from the cockroaches. I promised to stand guard over them through the night. They both went right to sleep. I snatched a few winks here and there, but deep sleep was impossible. The war with the roaches had pumped me full of adrenalin. I stood watch as promised, armed with a rolled up newspaper and ready to defend my babies. It was a long night.

Fortunately, the receptionist had allowed me to keep some milk in the hotel's refrigerator (I had the good fortune to never look inside it), so I had the makings of breakfast for Hunter and Ryan. Beyond that, I had nothing to eat and no money. I needed to find work immediately. Since my family would not help, I had to be assertive and bold. I fed the boys and took them with me to the front desk.

"May I ask you for a favor, sir?" I said humbly.

"Yes," the clerk replied, "what can I do for you?"

"Well, I'm a single mom. I have no money, and I need to look for a job. Do you think you could let me have a room for one more day? I promise to pay you later. I need a room for my babysitter to watch my babies for me while I find work." I noticed that his nametag said "Manager."

"It's all right," he said, "you can have room number 4A on the first floor. I won't charge you. It's on me." He took the key from its hook on a board behind him and gave it to me.

"Thank you, thank you so much," I said. I really felt like crying, but it did not fit the bold image I had put in mind for myself. I took the children, and we began to walk down Ferney Street. I was looking for a teenager, preferably someone I knew growing up in Dearborn; someone I could trust. We only walked a short way when I saw a familiar face walking toward us on the opposite side of the street.

"Debbie," I called as she came nearer. When she turned and waved, I motioned for her to come over.

"How are you, Debbie? How have you been?"

"Fine," she replied, "I haven't seen you in such a long time, Nadia. What's new with you?"

"I know, Debbie, I don't come here much anymore. There's so much to tell you, but I need a favor now." I told her about my breakup with Billy and that I was trying to make it on my own. "So, Debbie, can you babysit for me for about four hours at the Tuxedo Hotel? I have to look for a job. I'll pay you as soon as I make some money. Will you do it for me?"

"Sure, Nadia," she replied, "I'll do it for you."

"Thank you, Debbie," I said gratefully, "and one more thing." I hesitated to tell her, but I had to be honest.

"What's that, Nadia?" she asked.

"Keep an eye out for roaches. I didn't tell the manager about them, because I needed the room." No doubt he already knew.

"I'll watch," she said. I could see that she was not enamored with the idea, but I was confident that she would take good care of my babies.

I put Debbie in charge of Hunter and Ryan and set out to look for work. I checked on various jobs, but they only offered to pay minimum wage. I could not support my children earning a dollar and fifty cents an hour. Finally, after searching for a couple of hours, I came to a club that had a sign posted above the door: "Go-Go Dancers Needed." I stepped inside and went to the counter to enquire about the job. I knew nothing about go-go dancing, but I felt good about being able to do it because dancing was something I had enjoyed since I could walk. I danced to *American Bandstand* after school, to records after lunch in the school cafeteria, to the jukebox at Cunningham's Drug Store, and just about anywhere else. Dancing came naturally to me. How different could go-go dancing be?

The owner-manager named Frank immediately asked me to audition. "You're a very pretty girl with a nice figure," he said, "but let's see if you can dance. If you can, you'll make five dollars an hour plus your tips."

I stepped onto the stage and into the spotlight. Music began to play from speakers on the floor and the sides of the stage. I started to dance, pretty cautiously at first. The audience was all men, except for the two other dancers. I danced and did very well, I thought, until I came off the stage. Frank told me that, in fact, I did a great job, but I needed to look at the audience and smile once in a while.

"You never looked up once, and you never smiled," Frank said. "People come here to drink and see happy faces."

"I can do it, Frank," I said confidently. "I've never danced on stage before, but I can do it. Please give me a chance. I'm a single mom with two babies, and I need the money."

"All right, I'll give you a chance," he replied. "You're hired."

"Thank you, Frank, thank you so much." I looked over at the other two girls who had been watching me dance. They came and introduced themselves.

"Hi, I'm Tammy," said one.

"And I'm Mary," said the other.

"Ladies, this is Alisha," Frank said. "Nadia, this is your stage name from now on."

"Fine, Alisha is good," I replied. "Thanks again, Frank." I had a new name and a new job. Still, I had no money, and Debbie had to be paid. I also needed to find a safe place for my babies. I took a risk.

"Frank, I hate to ask, but I really need a favor. I'm going to get five dollars an hour to start. Would you give me a week's pay in advance? I need to buy groceries and bus fare, and, most of all, I need to find a safe place for my babies and me to live."

"You don't even have the basic necessities?" Frank looked surprised.

"No, Frank, I'm penniless," I explained. "I just left my lunatic husband who tried to kill me. I only want to be safe and take care of my babies. I have no money."

"What if you don't come back? How do I know you'll come to work?"

"I'm good for the money. I promise, Frank. I promise on my life. I'll be back tonight for work."

Frank calculated five hours a night for five nights at five dollars an hour and handed me a hundred and twenty-five dollars in cash on pure faith.

"You're an angel, Frank," I said, giving him a big hug. "You have no idea how much this means to me. The money will get me through the week and should be enough to rent a studio apartment. I'll see you tonight."

I almost floated out of the club. I returned to the hotel, paid Debbie for the day and hired her as my permanent sitter for the coming weeks. Then I went to the apartment building across the street from the hotel and rented a studio apartment. The rent was seventy-five dollars a month. The studio was far from luxurious, but it was safe and clean, and I was told that there were no roaches in the building.

I did well at Frank's. The money was good, and I enjoyed dancing. I took the city bus to work and back every night. I walked from the bus stop on Dix Avenue to Tuxedo Street between two and three o'clock every morning. I never thought of it as being unsafe, and I was never accosted at any time.

I became friends with the two young women who were dancers at the club. We were like Charlie's Angels, always there for each other, no matter what. If men annoyed us or said something improper, we always stood up for each other. They loved me, and I loved them. They could not believe that I had two children and that I was so naïve about life.

I discovered that Mary was a dyke. She had short hair like a boy, wore gobs of purple eye shadow, eyeliner, lipstick, and tiny pierced earrings. She was five feet eight inches tall, very cute, and very masculine. Tammy was a lesbian, too. She hardly wore makeup, but she really did not need it. She was beautiful. She was very feminine. Knowing these women made me aware of lifestyles other than my own. They gave me an education. They also were kind enough to drive me home at night, and soon they were picking me up to take me to work with them. I lived out of the way from where they lived, but not once did they complain. They insisted. They were concerned only for my safety and well-being. I loved those girls very much. Sadly, the last I knew of them was that Tammy ended up in a mental hospital. Mary and I used to go and visit with her. She was not there the last time we went. No one could tell us where she had gone. Ultimately, we lost touch with each other. To this day, I have not been able to locate Tammy or Mary. I will always be grateful for how they treated me.

After a few weeks at the club, Billy discovered where I was staying and came over to try to talk me into going back to him. For the hundredth time, I told him that I did not believe he would change, and I was not interested in more abuse.

"I've given you many chances," I said. "I leave and come back, but things stay the same. You always promise, but you never deliver. I can't deal with it anymore, Billy. I'm through. This time it's over for real. I have a good job and things are looking better for me. I can take care of my babies and myself. I don't need you." It was like talking to a concrete pillar.

Billy threatened me and told me he would see me dead before anyone else could have me. That being said, I decided to move as soon as I could, so he could never find me or see his children again. I feared that he might kill me. Then my babies would end up being raised by his family. Worse yet, he might harm them. That was not going to happen. I vowed to do whatever it took to keep Billy out of our lives.

I made plans to move the next day. I found an apartment in Redford, Michigan. It was a luxury apartment. I went from roach-filled rooms to the sixth floor of luxury. I was in heaven. I had never seen apartments like this, except on TV. I found a babysitter in the building, a woman in her forties who had a husband and two children. They were Irish by the name of O'Shea. They were kind, caring, and loving toward my children and me. I paid them fifty dollars a week to babysit in the evenings, and they agreed to let the boys sleep over. I wanted to pick them up in the morning so as not to break their sleep. It was a good arrangement, but it was so hard each night to leave them at the O'Shea's. We all cried whenever I had to leave, but I still had limited options. I never depended on social services to take care of my children. I always worked, but it was never easy.

I worked at Frank's club for several months before I found a job that paid more and was closer to my apartment. It was at an upscale club in Detroit. It was a lot larger than Frank's with a better clientele. I made enough money there to buy a better car as well as some nice clothes and things for the apartment. The owner's name was Larry La Ronda.

I loved the atmosphere of the club. The stage was round and in the center of the room. The guests were seated all around it. It was very intimate.

The crowds were thrilled with my performances. I choreographed them myself. I created my best sets with *Crimson and Clover* by Tommy James and the Shondells, *Time Has Come Today* by The Chamber Brothers, *Satisfaction* by The Rolling Stones, and *The Horse* by Cliff Nobles. The audiences gave me standing ovations. They always threw money onto the stage to show their appreciation. It was so great to be recognized and to receive the crowd's adulation.

While I was at La Ronda's, I became good friends with the bouncers. Larry was very good to his dancers and always had the bouncers escort us to our cars after work. One night, I went out to the parking lot alone. I was unlocking the car door when I was grabbed from behind. My assailant put his hand over my mouth, so I couldn't scream for help. He held me while another thug tied my hands behind my back and blindfolded me. They threw me into the back seat of their car. I heard only the two voices from the front seat as the car sped off into the night.

We drove for a long time. I was not allowed to speak. There was nothing I could do but try to stay calm and wonder what would happen next. Where were they taking me? Would they rape me? Would they kill me? What would they do?

Finally, the car slowed and stopped. The two guys carried me into a building, whether it was an apartment or a house I do not know, but once inside I heard four voices. They untied my hands so they could strip off my clothes. Still blindfolded, I was thrown onto a bed. I twisted and turned with all my strength, but strong hands held me down. I screamed for help, but they punched me in the face and told me to be quiet or else. I found the courage to speak quietly to them. I had been through a lot of "else" before.

"Please, don't rape me," I pleaded. "Please, don't hurt me! Please, I have two babies. They need me. I'm working to take care of them. Please, let me go. If you do anything to me, I could die. I have a blood clot. I'm not well. If you rape me, the clot might kill me."

"What do you mean?" one of them asked.

"I have a blood clot in my vagina that could kill me if you rape me."

They did not understand what I was talking about, but they got scared. They did not want to kill me. No one said anything for a minute or two. Then they took me off the bed and threw me onto the floor. They proceeded to punch and kick me. I could not tell how many men were beating me, but I know it was more than one. I really thought that they were going to beat me to death, but they finally stopped, tied my hands and feet again, and took me out to the car. They took me back to La Ronda's parking lot where they untied me and told me not to take the blindfold off until I counted to twenty. I heard the car doors slam, but I didn't know if all the men had left, so I counted. When I took the blindfold off, they were gone.

I do not know how I managed to get into my car and drive home. I had escaped with my life, but I was badly bruised and very sore. It was a struggle to move. I had two black eyes that were almost swollen shut, and my lips were cut and bleeding.

As soon as I was able, I called the police to make a report. I told them that I was blindfolded the whole time of the abduction, but I thought I might be able to identify the men by their voices. The police did not give me much hope of their capture, since I did not see the faces of the kidnappers.

I never returned to La Ronda's after the incident. I called Larry to tell him what happened and that I had to quit. He totally understood. He was such a nice man. He loved life and was good to everyone. He always made me laugh. He knew I did not drink, but once he told the customers that I liked screwdrivers. There were twelve screwdrivers waiting at the bar for me when I finished my set! He was such a clown.

Breakaway

About a month after I quit, I heard on the radio that a Mr. La Ronda was shot and killed during a robbery at his nightclub. I was devastated. I cried my eyes out for days. I was so sad for him.

I had become an excellent go-go dancer at La Ronda's, so after I healed from the beating by the kidnappers, I went to another upscale nightclub called the Inner Circle where I earned eight dollars an hour. Of course, my tips were mine to keep. I usually took home over a hundred dollars a night. What I liked about this upscale club is that both men and women, all professionals, came to see the shows. I was called a tantrum dancer. I wore Danskin dance bikini bottoms and tops under my dress, like the ones they wear now on *Dancing With The Stars*. Everybody loved it. It was very sexy, and I was earning more money than ever. I bought a used Cadillac, and I was driving toward a new life.

Free at last!
Free at last!
Thank God Almighty!
We're free at last!

MARTIN LUTHER KING JR.

Free At Last

W HEN I WAS A CHILD, IT WAS CUSTOMARY TO recite the Pledge of Allegiance in public schools. The entire class would stand, face the flag with our hands over our hearts, and say: "I pledge allegiance to the flag of the United States of America and to the republic for which it stands, one nation under God, indivisible, with liberty and justice for all." The Pledge was a daily reminder to me of two things.

First, the Pledge affirmed my status as an American. This was important to me, because I was born in Lebanon, and my Arab parents did not permit me to associate with American friends. My friends had freedom to associate with anyone; their associations were seamless—indivisible. I wanted to be American. I wanted to be like my friends.

Second, the Pledge promised liberty and justice for all. Since I did not have personal liberty and felt unjustly treated much of the time, the recitation of the Pledge was a daily encouragement to steadfastly believe that my dreams of freedom would come true. I liked to recite it.

I learned early on that freedom is not free. It comes at a high price. As a female in a male-dominated culture, I did not have control over my own life nor did I have equal rights. Victims of abuse do not have freedom. They live in daily bondage. They are oppressed in two ways. Their abusers actively oppress them as slave owners did slaves, and they are passively oppressed by a society that does not protect them and their rights.

As an adult, I learned that I was not alone in my struggles for freedom. I began to see parallels between the struggle for freedom from sexual abuse and domestic violence and other great freedom movements. In both the Civil Rights Movement and the Suffrage Movement, many Americans have had to work for their freedom at enormous cost (just as I did in my Arabic culture), constrained as they were by a society that deemed them to be second-class citizens. When Francis Bellamy wrote the Pledge of Allegiance in 1892, he originally intended to include the words *equality* and *fraternity.* He reportedly abandoned the idea because it was too controversial. Many people opposed equal rights for women and blacks. One could speak about liberty and justice for all, but not equality! And, of course, *all* meant all white males, but not all women or blacks.

As I write, many women and blacks still do not have equal rights, but they keep fueling their dreams, hoping that one day the bright sun of justice will pierce through the overcast skies of their oppression. It has been a long struggle, a long wait, and it continues. In some cases, black males have received civil rights before women. For example, the Fifteenth Amendment of the Constitution of the United States granted the right to vote to all citizens regardless of race, race but not gender. Thus, Thomas Mundy Peterson was the first African American to vote in a public election in 1870.

As for women, on the other hand, while they could vote in certain states (like New Jersey) and on occasion for special elections in some districts in other states, our nation did not endorse the right for them to vote until half a century later. The first woman to vote under the Nineteenth Amendment, the Suffrage Amendment, was Mrs. Marie Ruoff Byrum. She cast her ballot in Missouri on August 31, 1920.

To introduce this chapter, I quoted from Martin Luther King's famous *Dream Speech* delivered on August 28, 1963, at the Lincoln Memorial in Washington, D.C. Reverend King noted that a full century had passed since President Lincoln signed the Emancipation Proclamation to free slaves, but blacks in America were still "sadly crippled by the manacles of segregation and the chains of discrimination." King said on another occasion: "Change does not roll in the wheels of inevitability, but comes through continuous struggle. And so we must straighten our backs and work for our freedom. A man can't ride you unless your back is bent."

What is freedom? Anton Chekhov said that the most absolute freedom imaginable is the "freedom from violence and lies." Victims of abuse know this to be true. We have all struggled for freedom from violence and lies because in our hearts we believed there was a better way to live. Franklin D. Roosevelt put it this way: "We, too, born of freedom, and believing in freedom, are willing to fight to maintain freedom. We, and all others who believe as deeply as we do, would rather die on our feet than live on our knees." Abused people know that it takes a strong dose of courage to get up off your knees.

Freedom is born of courage. It cannot be otherwise. Robert Frost said: "Freedom lies in being bold." If you are abused, do not give up, brave heart! Freedom will come if you stay the course, but you must be bold. I like what Walter Cronkite, the longtime TV news anchor, said: "There is no such thing as a little freedom. Either you are all free, or you are not free." In the kingdom of freedom, all citizens are equally free, and no one is oppressed. Let freedom reign!

Freedom is the cornerstone of the building of your dreams. The road to freedom from abuse may be long and hard, but dreams do come true. I am living proof of that. They come true because of courage, "not standing idly by" while abusers have their way. Like dreams, freedom is always active, and it is demanding work. In the eloquent words of Dwight D. Eisenhower: "Freedom has its life in the hearts, the actions, the spirit of men [and women] and so it must be daily earned and refreshed—else like a flower cut from its life-giving roots, it will wither and die."

Freedom is not negotiable. Dreams cannot be fulfilled without it. As Reverend Jesse Jackson has rightly said: "No one should negotiate their dreams. Dreams must be free to flee and fly high. No government, no legislature, has a right to limit your dreams. You should never agree to surrender your dreams."

I can only add that no abuser has the right to steal your freedom or your dreams. As Abraham Lincoln wrote: "Those who deny freedom to others deserve it not for themselves." Thomas Jefferson also wrote: "No man has a natural right to commit aggression on the equal rights of another, and this is all from which the laws ought to restrain him." No one is free if they are oppressed.

Neither are they free if they are the oppressor. In the words of civil rights spokesman Frederick Douglass: "No man can put a chain about the ankle of his fellow man without at last finding the other end fastened about his own neck." Gaining freedom from abuse means that you also set your abuser free. Perhaps you have not thought of it this way before, but staying in an abusive situation enables the abuser to remain in his bondage. You may think that being a passive caregiver will change your situation, but you cannot be a caregiver to your oppressor without compromising both your freedom and his. To leave an abuser does not necessarily mean that your love for him has died. The opposite may be true: it is a supreme act of love to leave someone, if leaving will set him free.

True freedom enables you to leave the scene of abuse without a heavy heart, to fly toward your dreams. Freedom is the opportunity to be true to yourself, to take responsibility for your own life. No matter how severe the abuse you are taking, if you remember nothing of what this book is about, remember the following words of Victor Frankl, the Austrian psychiatrist who survived the horrors of the Holocaust. His great book, *Man's Search for Meaning,* has been a tremendous help to me. In it he writes: "We who lived in concentration camps can remember the men who walked through the huts comforting others, giving away their last piece of bread. They may have been few in number, but they offer sufficient proof that everything can be taken from a man [or a woman] but one thing: the last of human freedoms—to choose one's attitude in any given set of circumstances, to choose one's own way."

That is freedom in a nutshell: *to choose one's own attitude in any given set of circumstances, to choose one's own way.* I am choosing my own way now after years of postponing my dreams. Today I enjoy the blessings and rewards of winning a hard-fought battle against the bondage of abuse. I am living my dreams after years of struggling. I am working and training hard to be the best actress I can be. I am grateful for every door that is opening for me.

Surviving abuse hones the spirit and sharpens one's sensitivity to others, but in the end, I know that whatever distance I have travelled along the road to healing and happiness is not all because of me. I accept the crowd's applause for doing something worthy of it, but I also give credit to God and to those who immerse me now in love and support, who enjoy my freedom with me and encourage me to go on to the highest heights that my dreams will carry me. I am finally living the life that I have imagined! Free at last! Free at last! Thank God Almighty! I am free at last!

Part Four

Moving On

Breakaway

A Worm and Her Majesty

"While upon this earth I crawl,
Humbly to Thy face I call,
Not knowing when or where or whence
I came or what I shall be hence.

"In my present circumstances,
Part by choice and part by chances,
I am but a lowly peasant
Yearning for a life more pleasant.

"From leaf to leaf I labor daily,
Always burdened, never gaily.
Is this the only life for me—
Devouring earth, tree by tree?

"Surely from Thy high position,
Thou canst see my dire condition.
Canst Thou tell me, is there hope
Beyond my narrow, dismal scope?"

Breakaway

"I am not some distant fairy,"
Spoke the Monarch to this query.
"Real as real I sit beside you.
From this branch I too will guide you.

"For once I was just as you are—
From my condition just as far.
The route I took from that to this
Is known as metamorphosis.

"You have begun to make a start.
That yearning deep within your heart,
If nurtured properly will grow,
Until one day my form you know.

"It is by choice and not by chances
That you change your circumstances.
Who you are and what you do
Is in the end all up to you."

"Monarch Royal," asked the Lowly,
"Does it happen fast or slowly?
Does it hurt or is it painless?
Is there blood or is it stainless?"

Breakaway

"It is a process," said Her Highness.
"Pain there is and times of dryness.
If blood there be upon your brow,
Would you be better off than now?

"There is a price that must be paid—
Your life upon the altar laid.
To learn to live you have to die.
I cannot give you reasons why.

"If fear dissuades you on the way,
It is as worm that you will stay.
But if by faith you come to die,
You will become a butterfly.

Ah, nothing is too late
Till the tired heart
Shall cease to palpitate.

HENRY WADSWORTH LONGFELLOW

Leaving Time

I HAVE CHOSEN THE TITLE OF THIS CHAPTER FOR its double meaning. It is time to leave when the victim of abuse realizes that there is no other way to survive. She can put up with the abuse no longer, and the abuser will not change. When the time to leave has come, it is important to leave time to make arrangements for the future. This is the second meaning. The decision to leave is just a point in time. Leaving time is a process. It takes time to figure out what you will do to make your life and the life of your children safe and secure. You must have a plan, and you must carefully work it out, although your circumstances may be desperate.

I believe there are three main reasons why it took me so long to break away from Billy. First, I had experienced abuse at the hands of men since my childhood. My grandfather molested me sexually as a little girl; my father beat me routinely during my teenage years; my boyfriend whom I trusted raped me; other men attempted to rape me or use me to gratify their own sexual desires; and my first husband assaulted me for three years and tried to kill me. With the exception of my cousin Ginger's husband and a few other men like my uncle Hassan, I had not seen a good male role model. The men in my life either wanted to use me for sex or wanted to control me. In any case, I was merely an object to them.

I assumed it was normal for men to be cruel to women. I knew no other way. It was as though I lived in a house without windows. People who live exclusively in the dark will eventually go blind. If they leave after a long confinement, their eyes will hurt and it may take a long time to adapt to the light, but they will eventually see normally. Those who do not leave will never know what it is like to walk in the light. I stepped into the light, but the process of adjusting was not painless.

Secondly, I knew of no place to go if I were to escape. I had no options. My family had disowned me for religious reasons. I had no financial resources. I had two babies to take care of. Of course, I put the interests of my children above my own needs for security and safety. They needed the essentials of food, shelter, and clothing as well as the stability of a family unit. How could I provide these things as a single mom? How could I manage on my own?

Finally, fear is probably the universal reason why women who are abused do not leave their tormentors. Underlying the fear is a self-image that has been battered until the abused woman routinely feels like a victim, a disenfranchised, powerless victim— a song without a voice. This is the status that the abuser wants to inflict on the abused. It is a matter of power and control.

What do abused women fear if they leave? Most importantly, they fear that their abuser will find them and inflict even greater abuse on them or perhaps even kill them. It is so ironic. The instinct of self-preservation, the most basic and strongest of all drives, is the very thing that keeps a woman under the thumb of an abuser when it should cause her to flee.

Breakaway

It is very easy to rationalize the behavior of your abuser. I learned that this really means to make *rational lies* about who the abuser is. Abuse victims may delude themselves as I did for a long time. They believe that their tormentor will change, if only they wait long enough, if only they make the right adjustments to the abuser, if only they try to be better people themselves. Subconsciously, they take on the responsibility of changing the abuser, of making him a better person. It is wishful thinking in most cases. We do not live yet in the era when the wolf lies down with the lamb.

If they fail in this challenge, abuse victims may come to feel that they are responsible for the abuse itself. They may even feel guilty for the actions of the abuser. They may feel that they are themselves the cause of the abuse. In this state of mind, to balance what I have called the guilt-blame teeter-totter, they may think that they are unworthy of a better life and that they actually deserve the abuse they receive. There were times that I had these feelings, although I was unable to analyze them then. I was not even aware that the longer I endured abuse, the more I found myself on a downward spiral of a disintegrating self-image.

I believe these are the main reasons why I did not leave Billy and why most women do not find the courage to leave their abusers. I am sure there are many more. All these reasons may be summed up like this: there comes a time when you either leave or you find that your self image has been so destroyed that you no longer have the means or the power to choose to leave.

In short, timing is everything, and it is often the most difficult thing. I endured years of abuse and did not find the time to leave until an alarm went off inside my head. I finally came to the point where I was able to say, "It's over," and really mean it in my gut. I believe the alarm is different for everyone who is abused. I also believe the alarm always goes off. It is essential to listen for the alarm and to take the appropriate action. You cannot sleep through it.

Every life has its own rhythm. There is a right time for whatever is good in life. It is when the timing is right that you find true happiness. Only then can you live in harmony with yourself and others. Everyone is looking for happiness when they should be looking to get the timing right; happiness will follow. In the decisions of life, knowing *when* to act is just as important as knowing *how*.

I know this for certain: when the timing is not right, you are out of control. You lose your freedom to choose. You feel like you are in prison. You feel hopeless. You are at the mercy of other people or circumstances. You lose your identity. You lose your dreams. You feel trapped. When you feel this way, you can either give up or you can fight for your life.

I have chosen to fight.

I have been fighting all my life.

Fighting for survival.

Fighting for safety.

Fighting for security.

Fighting for freedom.

Fighting for my dreams.

Fighting to be me.

Fighting for time to do *my* thing.

The Lebanese poet Khalil Gibran wrote in a book entitled *Sand and Foam*: "No longing remains unfulfilled." I believe this to be true. If you persist in your dream, you *will* achieve it. It may take longer than you think, but it will happen. It is worth fighting for.

As long as I allowed myself to be bound by the chains of abuse, I never realized my full potential. As it turned out, not long after I left Billy and became a go-go dancer, I began to tap more of my creative abilities. I became an entrepreneur. I never knew I had the potential until I broke the chain of abuse.

I have never been the type of person who punches a time clock. I like my freedom too much, so, when go-go dancing went topless, I stopped working for someone else and went into business for myself.

I read the paper and found that belly dancing was the new craze. I thought that would be exciting for me, since I danced from the age of three at weddings and at home whenever possible. Belly dancing was in my blood. Beginning at an early age, Arab girls swivel our little hips and raise our tiny arms in the air, circling them around and around to the music. I decided to be a professional belly dancer. I had some experience already, and I had some good contacts. I was friendly with a few of the wives of the Detroit Lions football team. I gave them private lessons, and they had so much fun. They encouraged me. Gina, the best friend of my life whom I met at church when I moved to Troy, Michigan, was enthusiastic, too.

I revealed my plan to Gina: "I think I'll place an ad in the paper and see how much of a response I get, and then I'll go from there. I'll teach at home and charge five dollars an hour."

"That's great," Gina said, "if anybody can do it, you can." It was great to have her positive support. How I do miss her! She died of breast cancer fifteen years ago at the early age of fifty-eight, but she will always be my best friend. She always believed in me.

I placed the ad in the local paper and was surprised when I received a call from a school district about twenty minutes from where I lived. They wanted me to teach a six-week night course in beginning belly dance to adults. They would give me the biggest part of the tuition for each student. I agreed to do it. It was good money. I began the classes on Thursday nights. I had over a hundred women and teens sign up. We had to divide them into two classes. The two classes soon turned into three, and another night had to be scheduled.

Soon another school district heard about me and invited me to teach for them. Before long, I was driving four nights a week, teaching three to four classes a night at three different districts. Gina usually went with me. She was amazed at the number of students I had, and she was so happy for me. She saw my love for the dance. She also knew I was tired of the driving. I had to do something about it. Then I thought of a great idea.

The idea came to me when I was driving home one night. I decided to lease a building, start my own belly dance school, and have all the ladies come to me. I would drive no more than the distance from my home to my school. I would be able to set my own hours and make my own fee schedule. When I went to each district the following week, I asked my students how many would come to my school if I opened one up and gave them the dance classes at the same price? Almost all of them agreed to come with me. Some said it depended how far away I would be. I told them I would make it as convenient as possible for them. I decided to look for a studio right away.

Gina was so excited. "Nadia," she said, "you're doing the smartest thing ever. Now all your students will do the driving, and you'll just do what you do best—teach belly dancing."

"Does that mean I can't drive?" I teased, and we had a good laugh.

We found a building in Auburn Heights, Michigan, and it was perfect. It was a stand-alone building with two large windows. As usual, I was impulsive, got excited, and signed a lease for one year. I immediately had a sign made to put above the entrance. Gina and I contacted some of the women in my classes by phone to tell them about the new location. We also made announcements at the school district classes. I set the dates to open at my studio, and most of the women and teens came as expected. I knew they would, especially if I did not raise the prices. I charged the same for beginner and intermediate classes, but I raised prices for new students and for the advanced classes. The students were all very happy.

I was even happier. I had my own school of dance! One of my students was a seamstress who was willing to make costumes for all the girls. I bought the costumes at wholesale from her and sold them at retail. The seamstress's husband was a professional photographer. He took photographs of my students that I sold at a nice profit as well. They were a big hit with the students. I also found a source where I could buy belly dance albums. These made a profit also as the ladies bought them to practice. I opened a little shop in the studio and sold my students everything they needed. Who would have thought that I could earn so much money and have so much fun at the same time? I was doing exactly what I loved!

My next thought was that I wanted a house. I was twenty-three years old with two children and a second husband, but I had never been able to afford a house. I had recently married Little Bo of *Johnny and the Hurricanes* whom I had met at King Arthur's Club. With the success I enjoyed, I could actually build a new house and afford to pay cash for it. I was especially happy to give my boys a back yard and a basement where they could have parties and play with their friends on rainy days. I found a great builder in Troy, Michigan, the city next door to Clawson where I was living at the time. The city of Clawson was great, but Troy was where I really wanted to live. Troy was absolutely beautiful. Nature surrounded the area where I wanted to build. Troy was booming and Oakland County was the richest county in Michigan. I called the builder to set an appointment to meet and look at the lots that were available. I was thrilled with my new venture.

Mr. Rollan, the tall, easy-going owner of the construction company, worked with me from the beginning of the project. Since I was paying for the house, I wanted it my way. I was in control of the biggest project that most people undertake. I was stronger and happier than I had ever been. I paid Mr. Rollan for each installment of the work as it was completed: foundation, framing, roof, insulation and drywall, flooring, right to the finish. All the money came from my dance performances and belly dance classes.

Along with financial success, I also gained celebrity. I was making TV appearances and was a feature story for the *Detroit News* and the *Detroit Free Press*. I was in the papers almost every week. Soupy Sales called me from ABC and asked me to belly dance on his telethon to raise money for the March of Dimes.

The town of Clawson invited me to perform on a belly dance float in their Fourth of July celebration. I decided to give the float a harem theme. My students got involved and decorated the float with flowers and a harem's tent. One of the student's husbands acted as the sheik, and several of the dancers lounged with him in the tent. A stage was built for me in the center of the float where I could perform. Unfortunately, on the day of the parade I was ill with a fever of a hundred and two degrees, but, as the saying goes, the show must go on. I performed anyway, and the crowd loved it.

It was fabulous to have the support of my students in the dance school. I could not have done half of what I did without them. They motivated me and loved me. I had my own fan club: my students, their families, my band, and everyone else that made money from my business. I headlined at dinner clubs in the evening and encouraged my students to do the same. Some of them became regular performers at clubs and made a very good living at it.

After a while, the demands of my performing and teaching schedule began to take their toll at home. My husband felt uncomfortable that his wife was famous, making more money than he was, and not spending enough time at home. I compromised by closing up my studio but continued to perform in the evenings at dinner clubs all over Michigan. I also accepted invitations to perform for organizations like Optimist International and the Rotary Club. They always treated me well.

Apart from the occasional luncheon performances at the Optimist or Rotary Clubs, I was at home during the day until my sons came home from school. I made dinner for them and took them to their games and parties or wherever they needed to go. Spending time with them was always very important to me. Then I would leave around eight or nine o'clock in the evening to perform, usually doing two shows a night on Friday and the weekend. The money was good, but I worked hard for every nickel of it. I often thought of doing something else. Most of what I had done in life was a reaction in order to survive, to do whatever it took to make a good living and to put food on the table for my children. Now I was truly free to choose whatever I wanted to do.

I loved clothes, shoes, lingerie, etc., so one day I told my friend Gina that I had decided to open a boutique. I told her we could get all our clothes at wholesale and make a good profit on the retail end. Gina loved the idea. I invited her to go with me to Chicago to buy the merchandise for the store. We could not wait to go shopping together.

Getting the brand name right is always important for business. One day, while driving my sons to a soccer game, I asked them what they thought might be a good name for the boutique.

"Foxy Lady," Hunter said. Both boys liked Jimmy Hendrix, and so it was called Foxy Lady, except that I changed the spelling to *Foxee Lady* to give it a French flare.

So *Foxee Lady* was put together in just two months. I had noticed a little mall in Rochester, Michigan, that was absolutely perfect for a location. I called the number on the sign in the window and met with the owner who was a very handsome man in his thirties. His name was Ira Sabat. Ira and I hit it off immediately. He was very enthusiastic about my project, and he was a great help in getting things done the way I wanted them.

I leased a tiny three-hundred-square-foot space for three hundred dollars a month, and Gina and I went on a shopping spree in Chicago for sexy lingerie. We had a grand time! My first inventory consisted of long and short sheer gowns, sheer robes, baby dolls of all colors and sizes, crotchless panties, sexy mesh stockings, garter belts trimmed with ribbons, and sexy satin high-heeled slippers with feathers. This stuff was hot!

The folks in Rochester went wild about it. All kinds of people, both men and women, mobbed the store and bought every piece of inventory I had. The store was empty within a week of stocking it. I called my wholesalers and reordered the whole inventory again. *Foxee Lady* was a great success!

Ira noticed my ability to make money and asked me to go into business with him. Right across from *Foxee Lady*, we opened a store I called *Main Street Jeans*. We inventoried jeans of every brand you could think of, nothing but jeans. I operated both stores every day and hired two sales girls to help part-time. The jean shop was also a big success.

My businesses flourished. I had radio spots advertising my boutiques. I advertised in the papers. I had fashion shows for businessmen at upscale clubs where men bought the actual clothes worn by the models.

For years I maintained a hectic pace: running the stores, directing, narrating, modeling at the fashion shows, performing on weekends, and headlining at dinner clubs. The rest of the time I tried to spend at home with my boys. The truth is, I lost perspective. I was exhausted. I woke one morning to find that my body was numb. I could not get out of bed. I had lost the rhythm of my life. I was forcing everything to happen. Even success can be a kind of abuse if it takes away your health and your freedom.

Now, after many years of waiting, my dream to be an actor has come true. I have always wanted to act. Now I am a working actor, and I am a member of SAG (the Screen Actors Guild). I have a fabulous agent, my resume looks great, and I am continuing to train with great teachers. Even though I am only at the start of my acting career, I am thrilled to be doing it. Finally also, I have a husband who loves me and fully supports me in whatever I choose to do. I supported him during his career, and now he is supporting my dream. We have a wonderful marriage. We just celebrated our twenty-fourth anniversary.

My two sons are also supportive of me. Hunter and Ryan are men now. I am so proud of them. They are brilliant young men, and I love them both with all of my heart. We struggled together when they were children, and they were often the reason I was able to survive the challenges and obstacles I had to overcome. They needed me, and I needed them.

I must say that it took many years for me to heal, and the process is ongoing. Habits learned or behaviors practiced during years of abuse linger on. They work themselves out in the strangest ways, ways hard to understand. For example, it was only after many years that I came to like flowers and animals. Until then, I could not care less about receiving flowers as a romantic gesture. I thought flowers were ugly and meaningless. I did not see them as a symbol of love, and I had difficulty receiving love in any case. I had always been treated as an object. As far as I was concerned, gifts of flowers represented manipulation, control, and obligation. I wanted none of it. I only wanted my freedom. The victim of abuse has no context for love. Now I have a greenhouse in my backyard!

As for pets, I could not be bothered. I had no interest in them at all. They infringed on my independence. I did not want to be responsible to take care of them, nor did I want to be tied down. I had no appreciation for the love they give. I did not know that I had the capacity to love them. I have been transformed in my thinking through the years. I now love all of nature. I have had over fifteen indoor and outdoor cats through the years (all neutered and spayed, of course), and I always find homes for stray cats and dogs. I believe now that life is sacred for everything that breathes. You know you are healing from abuse when you can love the world around you.

It is my hope that this book has come into your hands at the right time for you. If you are locked into a situation of abuse, you need to consider when it is time to leave. You must know that your life is in danger. You need to look at your own dreams and give up the idea of being the one who rescues or forgives the abuser over and over again. The abuse is not your fault. You need to be yourself. You may require professional counseling as to whether you stay or leave. Please do seek professional help if necessary. Know yourself and be yourself.

If you have heard the beat of your own heart and learned to follow that rhythm with your choices, you are free. If you are still learning to listen, still struggling, still longing to realize your dreams, let the story of my life bring you hope. Just remember, it is never too late as long as you have breath. Remember my favorite lines from Longfellow: "Ah, nothing is too late, till the tired heart shall cease to palpitate." Never give up! Never give up!

Go confidently in the direction of your dreams;
Live the life you have imagined.

HENRY DAVID THOREAU

A Final Word

DOMESTIC VIOLENCE IS A GLOBAL PROBLEM. Statistics show that at least a third of the women in the world have been beaten or forced to have sex against their will, and the abuse and neglect of children is a problem of epidemic proportions. Someone is sexually assaulted every two minutes in America. I happened to be born in Lebanon to Arab parents who were Muslims in the Shia tradition. However, the experiences I have related in this book are not unique to my culture. The fact is that domestic violence occurs irrespective of culture or economic status the world over.

I endured a variety of abuses early in life and persevered to eventually realize my dream to be an actress. I am one of the fortunate ones. Many victims of abuse do not survive. Of those that do, millions are unable to repair the emotional damage done to them. The repair is ongoing. We are like flowers and trees. We have our seasons. Some seasons are more conducive to growth than others. Always we need care and nurturing. Recovery from abuse is a lifetime challenge. If you have been abused, I encourage you to never give up. Let your physical and emotional scars become the signs of your healing. Make good choices, be patient, and be positive about your progress.

For those of us who have experienced abuse, it is not necessary to define it. Abuse is a many-headed monster, and we are familiar with all its faces. We have seen them in the angry expressions of our abusers who wear them like masks in their violent moods and take them off when they resume their docile roles as our parents or lovers. We know the fear of living with the Jekyll and Hyde personality of an abuser. It makes life very fragile.

We know that life is fragile because we have been broken. We are not mere statistics. We are vital human beings whose lives have been shipwrecked, and we have been left the task of putting the pieces together. It is a lonely work usually done in silence. Abused children, in particular, innocent and helpless in a stormy sea of physical and emotional trauma, have no idea how to reconstruct the shape of their lives. There is a high probability that as adults they will repeat the kinds of abuse they received as children. Each generation adds a link to the chain of abuse until the force of a resolute will finally breaks the chain. Freedom from the bondage of abuse is a choice. It is an act of solemn will, but it is far from free. I have made the move to freedom, to new horizons, but I have paid dearly for it.

There are two kinds of abuse cases: those that are reported and those that are not. Of course, statistics reflect only cases that have been reported, and the numbers are astronomical. Actual cases are much more frequent than the statistics show and may be three to five times higher.

Because the subject of abuse is often shrouded in silence, it is important to highlight the horrible extent of the problem. Various surveys confirm the following statistics. For example, in America, although statistics vary depending on the method of survey, as many as three million women are physically abused every year, most often by a husband, boyfriend, family member, or other intimate. One-third of the women surveyed indicated that they had a female friend who had been assaulted by a significant other in the past year. Assaults by an intimate account for forty percent of the women treated in hospital emergency rooms.

Approximately seventy percent of rape victims know their assailants. An estimated 17.7 million women in America have been victims of attempted or completed rape according to RAINN, the Rape, Abuse & Incest National Network.

Each year approximately five hundred thousand women are assaulted during pregnancy by a spouse or other intimate. Pregnant women are more likely to die at the hands of their significant others than from any other major cause: more than cancer, motor vehicle accidents, or heart attacks.

Abuse of female students is very common. One female high school student in five has been physically or sexually abused by a date. Almost half of the girls surveyed knew someone who had been physically beaten by a boyfriend. One girl in ten admitted to having a boyfriend force her into sex against her will. Statistics show that four thousand girls are raped in high schools across America every year. Women of college age are four times more likely to be sexually assaulted than other members of the general population.

Rape is a common problem for married women as well. Three out of four adult women reported that their rape or rapes occurred at the hands of a spouse or former husband. Almost sixty-five thousand women are raped annually in America. That is the reported number. The real number may be as high as two hundred thousand or more.

Sadly, some women pay the ultimate price at the hands of their abusers. Whether their motives are intentional or not, significant others murder three women every day in America.

The abuse of children is also a problem of gigantic proportions. Their suffering continues unabated. More than three million cases of child abuse are reported every year. Again, it is estimated that the actual number of cases is three times greater or nearly ten million! Four children die every day as a result of child abuse, and three-fourths of these victims are under the age of four.

There is a report of child abuse every ten seconds. Inasmuch as the abuse of infants and children is most often done in private, the actual extent of their distress is unknown. If they survive, they either cannot tell their story or they do not speak out because of shame or fear of reprisal.

The costs associated with domestic violence and sexual abuses are sky high. For example, the cost of medical care for women who have been raped or assaulted is estimated at six billion dollars annually in the United States. It is impossible to estimate the cost to society for treating victims who do not receive medical attention. Many abused women manage their own physical and emotional wounds, but there are still other costs involved. Vast sums of money are spent on prisons to incarcerate and rehabilitate sexual predators and abusers. The cost of intervention by police and social workers is enormous. The actual sums spent directly on rehabilitation of abused children do not reflect the total picture, since children often do not gain access to professional help.

However, the cost to society multiplies when a significantly high percentage of abused children become abusers themselves as adults. According to RAINN statistics, victims of sexual assault are three times more likely to suffer from depression, six times more likely to suffer from post-traumatic stress disorder, thirteen times more likely to abuse alcohol, twenty-six times more likely to abuse drugs, and four times more likely to contemplate suicide. There is simply no way to calculate the high cost of abuse in our society. Abuse is an economic drain on all Americans.

The sexual molestation of children is a shadow on the land of America. Only those of us who have survived it know the depths of despair that it brings. There are multitudes of us who have suppressed or repressed the agony of molestation and committed it, whether consciously or unconsciously, to a grave of silence. The grizzly details may be resurrected and the trauma dealt with later in life as in my case, but many women take the torture of abuse to their own graves without ever being freed of the burden. The mental and emotional baggage they carry has a profound effect on their lives. Being molested as a child is a common reason why many women do not trust men. Relationships suffer because feelings of intimacy, both sexual and emotional, may be blocked by the trauma they experienced as girls. The monster of abuse lives on, but it is not always recognized as the root of relational problems.

What is to be done? Three things are needed: passion, patience, and persistence. First and foremost, let there be a passionate outcry from the public against abuse. Let the people open their eyes and ears to the cries of the oppressed. Let us no longer keep our silent vigil over the suffering around us. Media and public figures need to focus attention on the topic of abuse, not just for a day, a week, or a month, but routinely. Politicians need to put it on their agendas. Parents need to be passionate about the protection of their children. People in general need to be educated about the horrors of abuse and encouraged to intervene when they confront it. Legislators must make laws that will deter domestic violence and sexual abuse, and judges must impose on convicted abusers and sex offenders the strictest penalties available under the law.

Some progress has been made in the legal arena. The Violence Against Women Act of 1994 designates $1.6 billion to facilitate the investigation and prosecution of violent crimes against women. The International Violence Against Women Act of 2007 addresses global domestic violence. The Protect Our Children Act, already approved by the House of Representatives, is pending in the United States Senate. If it becomes law, it will provide $320 million over the next five years to provide funds to fight sexual exploitation of children on the Internet. These and other legislative measures are positive steps forward.

Unfortunately, in June 2008, the United States Supreme Court ruled against capital punishment as a fit penalty for the rape of children. While four justices dissented vehemently, the majority held that the punishment was too severe for the crime. The decision seems to favor the criminal more than the victim; the life of the child is devalued once again. The Court, in my view, is out of touch with the reality of the suffering that is endured by the raped child. It is a sad day in America when the highest court in the land fails to protect innocent children.

The ruling held that murder alone deserves capital punishment, but what the Court failed to understand is that there are many ways besides murder to take the life of a child. The rape of a child cannot be viewed as a single event. It must be seen as the beginning of the victim's lifelong struggle to deal with the emotional and physical pain caused by being violated. All too often, the victim is ignored by our judicial system while the focus is entirely on the criminal and his so-called rights. Even when offenders are apprehended, statistics show that only six percent of rapists spend time in jail, the rest are set free to walk the streets. If the courts of our land will not defend the rights of children, who will?

Unless society changes, abuse will not be banned from the scene of American life. Freedom from physical and sexual abuse should be an inherent right of all our people, a right defended by every citizen in every place in our great land and especially in our courts.

The healing of America cannot be accomplished overnight. Protecting innocent victims against violence will require patience and persistence as well as passion. Abuse will continue until our society wages a conscious, continuous, purposeful, and passionate fight against it.

Offenders should be made to pay for their crimes and not merely by incarceration. How they should pay is an open question. I believe that victims should receive reparations from sexual offenders, but even if compensation were to be made, it would not be sufficient. Who can measure the value of a life stolen at the age of four or five? Who can lift the emotional burdens from the victims of abuse? Who can erase the memories that are indelibly etched on the mind of the assaulted? Who can compensate a woman for dreams that have been dashed to pieces, careers that have been ruined, hopes that have never materialized, wounds that have never healed, and scars that cannot be removed? Who, we must ask, can do the impossible?

I found the answer to these questions in my faith, for I believe that only God can do the impossible. I was lost in a slough of despair when God's love rescued me. His love lifted me and carried me through difficult times toward the realization of my dreams. His grace and mercy saved my life on several occasions. I have experienced the miracle of healing in the face of death.

I believe that we are all God's children, and I know that God protects us, but many women do not have such faith. What will they do? How can they cope? It would be better by far that they should never have to face the reality of needing a miracle to go on with their lives.

Shall we continue to allow abuse to define the culture of America? How can we say that we live in a civilized society when women and children are treated like mere objects, forced into sex acts against their will, humiliated, beaten, bruised, broken, hospitalized, and yes, even murdered? How can we say that we are civilized when these acts of violence against women and children are committed with impunity in our country every day, year after year? How can we survive as a nation if we do not find a solution to the endless mistreatment of more than half our population, the very women who give birth to each succeeding generation and the children who will inherit our legacy?

Now is the time for action. It is time to speak up and to stop putting up with abuse. We sing about our country as the "land of the free and the home of the brave," but victims of abuse know that they have no freedom. On the other hand, they understand too well what it means to be brave. Out of necessity, they muster courage virtually every day of their lives to cope, to dream, to hope that tomorrow might be better and free of pain. They receive no Purple Hearts for their injuries; they move forward into the next battle unrewarded and unrecognized for their valor. They are truly courageous, and when they are free of abuse there will be meaning for them in the national anthem. Let the masses of abused victims sing the song of freedom!

If you are fortunate to have lived free of abuse, please know that there are many around you who have not. Do not stand idly by while others are being oppressed. Get involved. Let the reading of my story be your catalyst to join those of us who are fighting against domestic violence and sexual abuse. We need your help. We can end the scourge of abuse in America. We can do it together!

To err is human, to forgive divine.

ALEXANDER POPE

Epilogue

I FILED FOR DIVORCE AFTER I LEFT BILLY, AND IT was final a year later, the minimum waiting period in Michigan at the time. I did not want to see him again after he threatened to kill me when I was working at Frank's as a go-go girl. I moved to Redford, Michigan, and kept right on moving. I was afraid that he might carry out his threat. I was not worried so much about what he might do to me, but I meant to protect Hunter and Ryan at any cost. I always kept them with me. If ever Billy were to find us, he would have to hit a moving target.

The United States was embroiled in the Vietnam War then, and it was not going well. The war started in 1954 and continued until 1975. U.S. military advisors were involved in Vietnam since the early 1950s to help prevent a communist takeover of South Vietnam. The first combat troops were sent in 1965. As the war effort progressed poorly under President Johnson, military recruiters found it difficult to fill their quotas. On December 1, 1969, the Selective Service System instituted the first draft lottery since 1942. Some eight hundred and fifty thousand young men between the ages of nineteen and twenty-five were to be inducted into military service. The lottery was based on birth dates. Deferments were given for college students, heads of households, and others, so single men were the most likely to be drafted.

Since the divorce ended Billy's head of household status and he was not in college, he stood to be drafted if his number came up. Unfortunately, his birthday put him near the top of the list. He was informed that he would either have to enlist, or he would be drafted. Billy chose not to enlist, so he was caught in the net of the lottery. Billy was going to war.

Coincidentally, I saw Billy at the processing center on the day he was shipped out. I happened to be there to say goodbye to a friend. Billy was there with his girlfriend. We greeted each other cordially, but he was obviously nervous. I cried for him that day, because he would not have been drafted if we had remained married. I felt very guilty.

After that, I had no contact with Billy until I decided to find him. Hunter and Ryan were already in their late twenties, and I was happily married finally. Of course, the boys had no recollection of their biological father, since they were both babies when I left Billy. They never asked me to contact Billy, but I wanted to know if he had medical issues that might in some way impact the boys. I contacted authorities in the city where I thought he might be, and, after a thorough investigation, I was able to locate him.

My husband and I were living in the Chicago area at the time. It was just before Thanksgiving when I drove to the Detroit area to visit Billy. I found him living in a small room in a halfway house. He had no possessions, not even a winter coat. The room lacked a kitchen and a bath. A single bath in the hallway served all the men in the house. Billy had space for only his bed, a small table, and a closet. Ironically, Billy's living situation was not unlike my grandfather's room in some ways. Billy was eating something out of a tin can when I arrived, something heated on a hotplate. The beer bottles on the windowsill indicated that he still was a slave to alcohol. Although not quite fifty years old, he looked very worn and tired, the effects of a lifetime of alcohol and substance abuse were clearly written on his face.

While there is much more to tell about my reunion with Billy, I need to underline briefly the importance of reconciliation to the healing process. Unlike my grandfather and my father, neither of whom confessed their wrongs, Billy was very contrite. He was genuinely surprised and happy to see me, but, after he recovered from the initial shock, he broke down.

"Nadia, I'm so sorry for everything I did to you." His confession was sincere and real. His tears flowed freely as he unburdened a heart that had been carrying a load of guilt for more than twenty-five years. "I'm so sorry, Nadia. I was a fool. I was just a stupid kid, but it shouldn't have happened anyway. I should never have hurt you. I'm so sorry. Everything was my fault. Please forgive me."

"It's okay, Billy, I understand, and I do forgive you. Thank you for asking, but it's all in the past. I'm glad I came here today. Do you want to see pictures of your children?"

"Sure, Nadia, of course." I could see that he was both eager and a little anxious at the same time. The last time he saw them, Hunter was a toddler, and Ryan was just a baby.

I sat with Billy at the little table in his little room and showed him his children. He was so humbled when he saw them, but I could see also that he was very proud. He practically flooded the room with tears, tears of joy for how handsome and good-looking his sons were, and tears of sadness for all the years he had lost without seeing them. He had missed their entire lives.

When I left Chicago, I had no idea how the reunion with Billy would go. I did not anticipate the effect it would have on me. Billy did not have any medical conditions that might have impacted Hunter and Ryan. There were no diseases or conditions he could give them. In fact, he had nothing to give them at all. He was by all accounts an empty vessel, but he gave me something profound and completely unexpected. By asking for forgiveness, he enabled me to release a reservoir of pain that I had stored up inside of me for years. I could not stop the flow of tears. The floodgates of my heart opened, and I cried until I could cry no more out of sheer exhaustion.

I bought Billy a winter coat and took him to dinner and gave him some cash. There was nothing else I could do for him. There was no way I could repay him for what he gave me that day. I drove back to Chicago renewed and refreshed.

Reconciliation with Billy set me free.

Reconciliation with my father never happened, because it requires confession and forgiveness. He died of heart failure in 1996. I attended the funeral. It was a dark affair. The mosque was crowded with people, most of whom I had never seen before, as they were not related to our family. Groups of women, completely covered in black *burkas* or the traditional *hijab,* wailed and beat themselves as a sign of grief. Above their laments, a tape of the Qur'an blared over the sound system.

My father's casket lay open at the front of the auditorium. It was almost ignored in the midst of the lamenting by the women and the speeches by various sheiks. It sat like a potted plant in the corner of a room. The ceremony went on nonstop for twenty-four hours. I did not participate in it. I felt very out of place. In the midst of the noise, I took time to sit quietly and look at my father's casket from a distance. I did not want to go up to view him.

I recalled the years of abuse that I had received at his hand as a teenager. I remembered feeling like a black sheep in my family after my parents disowned me. I relived the day that my father dragged me into the basement and tried to kill me. I felt the same remoteness from him in death that I had in life, a remoteness reinforced by my father whenever I visited him as an adult. I always hugged and kissed him, but he always pushed me away. We were never close. We never talked about it. My father was not a communicator. I never hated him, but I really felt no sadness at his passing. I felt nothing at all until I decided to do something about it. Eventually, I got in touch with my true, deep feelings.

I left my chair and walked slowly to Baba's casket. I stood before it for a long while looking at his lifeless, wax-like face, trying to think of something to say. Finally, a tear broke and the words flowed freely like a fountain from the depths of my heart, washing it free of painful memories:

I need to talk to you, Baba. This is Nadia, your eldest daughter. You never listened to me when I was growing up, but I hope you can hear me now.

I cannot forget what you did to me as a teenager. You never gave me a chance to prove that I could be trusted to make good decisions for my life. You never gave me the love and support I needed and deserved as your daughter. My heart aches when I think that I received beatings and curses from you instead of hugs and blessings.

More than anything, I wanted you to love me. I wanted to hear you say it, Baba, but you never did. Not even once. I wanted you to show it, but you could not. But I want you to know that I understand. You never had love as a child. You could not give what you never received. I believe that you loved me in your own way, Baba, but you had no idea how to show it. I understand and I forgive you.

I forgive you for the beatings. I forgive you for never showing love to me. I'm sorry that we never had the love that we both needed from each other. But I'm telling you now, one last time, hoping that you will believe me: I forgive you, Baba, and I love you.

I know it's hard for you to receive love, but please take my love and forgiveness with you on your journey. Keep them in the handbag of your heart as my gift to you. Let them bring you happiness, and remember me, Baba. This is Nadia, your eldest daughter.

Good-bye, Baba. God bless you, and may your soul rest in peace. I will always love you.

Seek not, my soul, the life of the immortals,
But enjoy to the full the resources that are
Within thy reach.

PINDAR

Resources

*N*UMEROUS RESOURCES ARE AVAILABLE NOW through governmental and non-governmental agencies as well as on the Internet to provide education and assistance for victims of abuse. Of the many resources I have consulted in writing the chapter entitled *A Final Word*, a select few are listed at random below. If you are in an abusive relationship, I encourage you to visit these and other sites, including chat rooms where you can share your concerns with others without cost or fear of reprisal. If you must do your research secretly, be sure to erase the history of your searches in your browser. Seek help and dare to make the move. Believe with all your heart that you can be free, and you, too, can become a butterfly! And don't forget faith. I have found that my faith in God has been my greatest resource.

If you are interested in contacting me, please go to my website at www.nadiasaharibook.com. Here is a random selection of some websites that provide useful information:

http://www.ojp.usdoj.gov/

The U.S. Department of Justice Bureau is a comprehensive resource for victims of crime. The Bureau of Justice Statistics reports comprehensive data on all types of abuse. See especially the very important National Crime Victimization Survey.

http://www.rainn.org/

The Rape, Abuse & Incest National Network reports statistics and provides resources to educate the public about sexual violence. It claims to be the nation's largest anti-sexual assault organization. Call the confidential 24/7 hotline at 1-800-656-HOPE.

http://joetorre.org

The Joe Torre Safe At Home Foundation serves to educate children about domestic violence so that they understand they are not alone and there is hope.

http://www.prevent-abuse-now.com/

This site presents articles, news, research and statistics sponsored by Dr. Nancy Faulkner's *Pandora's Box: The Secrecy of Child Sexual Abuse.*

http://www.acf.dhhs.gov/

The U.S. Department of Health & Human Services Administration for Children and Families promotes economic and social well-being of children and families, including services to prevent child abuse and neglect.

http://www.childwelfare.gov/can/prevalence/

This site provides state and national statistics from over seventy agencies about various types of abuse, maltreatment, and neglect.

http://ndas.cwla.org/

The Child Welfare League of America aims to be "The most comprehensive collection of national child welfare and related data."

http://www.fedstats.gov/

This site gives current statistics on just about everything from various agencies including the FBI, the Bureau of Prisons, and the Bureau of Justice Statistics.

http://www.ndacan.cornell.edu/

The National Data Archive on Child Abuse and Neglect provides current data for all states and promotes academic research and sharing of information on child maltreatment.

http://www.ispcan.org/

The International Society for Prevention of Child Abuse and Neglect claims to be "the only multidisciplinary international organization that brings together a worldwide cross-section of committed professionals" to prevent cruelty to children in every nation.

http://www.childstats.gov/

This site reports key indicators on children's lives, including child maltreatment and trends collected from twenty-two Federal agencies. Read the full report entitled *America's Children: Key National Indicators of Well-Being* for 2007.

http://childhelp.org/

CHILDHELP is a coalition of law enforcement, social, medical, and counselor services founded in 1959. The national child abuse hotline 1-800-4-A-CHILD operates 24/7.

http://childmolestationprevention.org/

Learn here the facts about child molestation and what you can do about it. Download research articles and publications.

http://www.lawyersforchildrenamerica.org/

Lawyers provide pro bono assistance to protect the rights of children who are victims of abuse.

http://endabuse.org/

This site provides a valuable resource on domestic violence sponsored by the Family Violence Prevention Fund. Click on the Resources tab and then Get the Facts.

http://www.nccev.org/

The National Center for Children Exposed to Violence at Yale University aims to increase the capacity of individuals and communities to reduce the incidence and impact of violence on children and families, to train professionals who intervene and treat victims of violence, and to increase public awareness of the effects of violence.

http://www.safeplace.org

In Austin, Texas, SafePlace "exists to end sexual and domestic violence through safety, healing, prevention, and social change."

http://www.safehavente.org

SafeHaven provides shelter facilities, counseling and legal services, education, 24-hour hotline interventional and other services to women and children affected by domestic violence in the greater Dallas/Fort Worth Area.

http://www.protect.org/

PROTECT is a national membership organization with a mission to protect children from abuse, exploitation, and neglect.

http://www. thefacefoundation.org

Established in 1995 by Russell W. H. Kridel, MD, of Houston, Texas, The Face Foundation provides surgical care at no fee to financially disadvantaged survivors of domestic violence who need restorative or reconstructive facial plastic surgery. Surgery on battered women is done in conjunction with a program sponsored by the National Coalition Against Domestic Violence and the American Academy of Facial Plastic and Reconstructive Surgery and its Face-To-Face program. The National Domestic Violence Program screens patients at 800-799-7233. Some three hundred and fifty surgeons are involved in this program.

http://www.missingkids.com/

The National Center for Missing & Exploited Children (NCMEC), established in 1984, exists to help prevent child abduction and sexual exploitation, to help find missing children, and to assist victims of child abduction and exploitation. NCMEC provides educational information, training programs for service professionals, legislative help, etc.

http://www.vaw.umn.edu/

Violence Against Women Online Resources was founded in 1997 to give web access to products funded by the Violence

Against Women Act. The online document library has extensive resources on advocacy, child protection, and criminal justice.

http://policyalmanac.org

The Almanac of Policy Issues is a comprehensive resource for archives on many issues, including domestic violence and law enforcement relating to sex crimes.

http://child-abuse.com

The site of the Child Abuse Prevention Network provides resources and training for professionals working in the field of child abuse. Considerable space is given to bibliographies for resources on how to manage the rehabilitation of abuse victims.

http://www.ndvh.org

The National Domestic Violence Hotline is available 24/7 to provide crisis intervention, safety planning, information, and referrals to agencies in all fifty states. The number to call is 1-800-799-SAFE (7233) or for the hearing impaired 1-800-787-3224 (TTY).

http://www.counselcareconnection.org

CounselCare Connection provides guidance and resources from a Christian perspective by licensed professionals on a variety of issues, including sexual abuse, anger management, child abuse, self-esteem, depression, suicide, etc. Referrals are made to the American Association of Christian Counselors.

http://www.aacc.net

The American Association of Christian Counselors is an umbrella organization set up to equip clinical, pastoral, and lay care-givers with little or no formal training to more effectively minister to those in need. The Christian Care Network is the referral organization for counselors nationwide.

http://www.burstingthebubble.com

This is a user-friendly website where young people can learn about what abuse is and how to deal with it.

http://www.standupforkids.org

This organization provides an outreach program for abused teens, including a safe environment to rest, referral services, educational assistance, counseling, etc.

http://www.mdjunction.com

This site offers online support groups relating to teens and sexual abuse.

http://www.survivorshealingcenter.org

Located in Santa Cruz, CA, SHC "provides education, information, referrals, quality services, and support to survivors of childhood sexual abuse and their allies."

http://www.ncvc.org

The National Center for Victims of Crime provides tools for teens (and others) on child sexual abuse, dating violence, sexual assault, stalking, bullying and harassment, etc.

http://wadt.org

Women Are Dreamers Too is a non-profit organization that aims to assist women who are victims of domestic violence, especially those who want to become economically self-sufficient.

http://youreworthit.org

The Women's Organization of Rebirth Through Healing "seeks to address and raise international awareness surrounding issues such as HIV/AIDS, sexual violence, displacement, personal safety, access to health care, food and shelter, detention, and gender discrimination."

http://www/ncadv.org

The National Coalition Against Domestic Violence works to eradicate social conditions that lead to domestic violence.

http://usattorneylegalservices.com/texas-women-shelters.html

Texas Women Shelters provide safety and protection to victims of domestic violence, especially low-income women who lack resources to find help elsewhere. This important site lists contact information for shelters throughout Texas.

http://www.vday.org

V-Day is a global movement to end violence against women and girls.

http://www.taasa.org

The Texas Association Against Sexual Assault is committed to ending sexual violence in Texas through education, prevention, and advocacy. For twenty years, TAASA has worked "to assist sexual assault survivors and to create a Texas free from sexual violence."

Discussion Questions

1. How do you relate to the story of Nadia's early life? Have you been the victim of abuse? How did you survive it?
2. Before reading *Breakaway*, were you aware of the terrible extent of domestic violence and sexual assaults in our country and worldwide? What can you do to help prevent domestic violence and sexual abuse?
3. Did you keep silent for a long time about your abuse? When were you first able to talk about it? Has reading Nadia's story given you courage to talk about it now?
4. Nadia writes that, "Recovery from abuse is a lifetime challenge." What specific steps can victims of abuse take to bring about emotional healing?
5. Can you define domestic violence? Would you intervene on behalf of someone you know that is being abused? What would you do about it?
6. What questions would you ask a child whom you suspect is being molested? What do you feel is your responsibility to educate others regarding domestic violence and sexual abuse?
7. Do you agree with the Supreme Court decision to ban capital punishment for the rape of children? Do you think their decision will deter sexual offenders? What is the appropriate punishment for sexual crimes?

8. At a certain point, Nadia said, "It's over." Did she wait too long? What gave her the courage to leave? When is the right time to leave an abuser? What precautions should be taken?
9. Nadia quotes Henry David Thoreau as saying, "Go confidently in the direction of your dreams; live the life you have imagined." What are your dreams? What is the life that you imagine for yourself?
10. Nadia played two roles as a child: Little Mother and Dream Girl. How do parents rob children of their childhood?
11. How did you react to the chapter entitled *Grandfather's Room*? What emotions did it elicit? Do you feel it is safe to leave a child alone under adult male supervision?
12. What key actions did Nadia take to achieve her freedom?
13. Do you know anyone like Nadia's father or husband? Is it ever right for a man to strike a woman or a child?
14. How did Nadia support herself after leaving her abusive husband? What would you have done in her case?
15. What should teenage girls do to protect themselves from date rape and other forms of assault?
16. What precautions should be taken to prevent molestation, abduction, and rape?
17. Do you think Nadia was right to put crazy Leon in jail? When is incarceration the right sanction for assault or sexual abuse? Why are only six percent of convicted rapists incarcerated?
18. How do you feel about Nadia's not allowing her children to see their father? What rights does the abuser have?
19. Are you a person of faith like Nadia? How has your faith helped you to heal from abuse?
20. Will you join Nadia in supporting legislation to ban abuse? Will you take the time to write to your legislative representatives?

Breakaway

Here's your chance to ponder deeply
On the things you're going to do
By the hour, day, or weekly—
Many things or just a few.
Think of children, helpless babies,
Think of women suffering, too.
They need commitment, not just maybe's.
Who will help them if not you?

Notes:

Notes:

Notes:

Notes: